# Program Your Micros POS System

Ver. 1v8

POS Lifeline.com

# Setting the Tax Rate .............................................................. 71

# Working with Employees in the Micros System ....................... 73

# Working with Jobs .................................................................. 89

# Employee Classes .................................................................. 94

# Changing the Bartender Speed Screen ................................... 107

# <u>General Introduction</u>

This book is designed to help the Business Manager as well as the Floor Manager. It is designed to literally walk a person through each programming step for a given task. It is illustrated with as many screenshots as possible to give the user a visual reference to go along with the step-by-step instructions. The purpose of all the screenshots is to instill confidence in the user who is new to programming a Micros POS system and not necessarily a computer wiz.

A properly maintained Micros POS system will translate into far more efficient reporting, inventory control and most importantly, customer service. The more time a server spends searching through menus for the correct item the less time they are able to spend on the floor with their customers. The effect of this is considerable. Customer service is compromised and the ability to up sell or turn a table more quickly is greatly reduced. In a busy environment the wrong orders become wasted product. When a new employee is hired they are required to learn a new menu and sometimes a new system. Having the POS system uniform and maintained allows the new employee to concentrate on the menu and their customers, not the process by which they communicate with the kitchen or the bar.

The programming that is covered in this book may seem pretty basic at first glance. But once you work through something like setting up a new special, you'll find that there are a number of small changes you can put together to make your life easier when it comes time to run payroll reports, sales journals or take an inventory.

In short, this book provides not only a step-by-step guide to the basics of Micros programming, it also serves as a reference that you can rely on for years to come.

POS Lifeline.com

# Introducing the Different Micros Programs

The Micros interface is made up of a number of different programs. Each of these programs serves a particular function to help the day manager or the Business / General Manager.

Micros Control Panel

This utility starts and stops all the services of the 3700 system. This is where operations are turned OFF before a system shutdown or ON after a start up or re-started in the event of a service failure. You can open this application at any time to see the status of every terminal in the restaurant.

Autosequences & Reports

This application is where the majority of the reporting is done. Besides the reports that run automatically, any information that you need to pull out of the database system is accessible through this application.

Manager Procedures

This application allows the user the ability to change menu items on the fly (such as pricing, availability and required condiments) from both the back of the house computer and the terminals. Primarily this is used for changing time card records because in most instances it is quicker to edit menu items through the POS Configurator.

POS Configurator

This is the main program that allows the user to modify the database. Through this program you can work with employees, menu items, tax tables, screen configurations, etc. This is where 90% of your Micros programming time will be spent. This book deals primarily with working with this program.

Credit Card Batch

This is a program that acts as the intermediary between the database (register system) and the banks to ensure payment has been processed and settled. The user will probably not use this very often but we will cover it briefly because should you need to, it is very important that you are familiar with how to navigate through it.

Transaction Analyzer

Transaction Analyzer is a program that creates reports by polling the transaction detail from the database. It allows you to sort through the data stored in the system based on operator defined fields. It allows the user to set conditions on a search and pulls out the required information. This is useful for tracking contests among the staff or looking for something particular. Please note: Transaction Analyzer only accesses data for the previous 14 days (prior to version RES4.1hf3). So if you're running a month long sales contest with the staff it is necessary to run it two or more times throughout the month to track the correct sales data.

EJ Organizer

Perhaps no program besides POS Configurator gets as much use as the EJ Organizer. This is a small but powerful utility that enables you to carefully step through the logs of every interaction with the POS system for a given day.

Every night, as part of the system's auto run utilities, Micros creates a backup ZIP file of the "register tape" for the previous day. This file includes every check and transaction from the night before. EJ Organizer is designed to be able to look at this register tape and quickly find relevant information. This program can be used for responding to charge backs from the bank, looking at how employees are entering food and drink orders and even as a safety check to identify theft.

Re-Boot Registers

This is a small utility that allows the back office manager or General Manager the ability to reboot each register on the system remotely. In a large installation this allows the weekly re-set to be completed easily and efficiently. Once the restaurant database has been shut down, this utility can be run and then the back office server can be restarted. For a detailed explanation see the discussion on the Control Panel which follows.

# Micros Control Panel

This utility starts and stops all the services of the 3700 system. This is where operations are turned OFF before a system shutdown or ON in the event of a service failure. You can open this application at any time to see the status of every terminal in the restaurant.

To start the Control Panel double click on the icon on the desktop:

That will open up a box similar to the following:

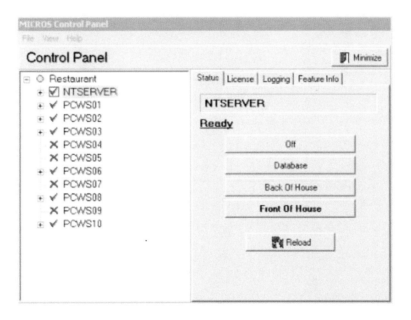

In the example above you can see that the restaurant has 10 workstations. Green checks indicate that the database has started and that particular workstation or server is fully operational.

Red X's indicate that the register or workstation is not operational. In the example above workstation #4, 5, 7 & 9 are not operational. (PCWS stands for PC workstation).

The system is configured so that if the system needs to be rebooted the Control Panel will automatically start up to the "Front of House" level and all services should come back as green check marks.

For normal service all workstations should have a green check mark next to them and the header ("Restaurant" at the top of the list) should have a green check mark as well.

**Re-Loading the Database**

Occasionally it will be necessary to re-load the database. This might be necessary if you've done a good deal of programming before opening for the day or if there was a system crash and short of re-booting the entire system, a re-load of the data base will suffice.

In order to reload the database click on the small plus ("+") mark next to NTSERVER. This will expand the viewable information for the server. The control panel should look something like this:

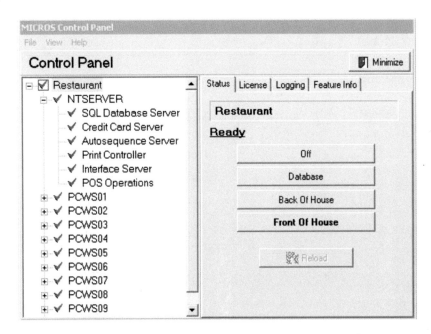

Notice that when we click the "+" button the various options for that particular machine are shown. For the server we see the Database Server (SQL Database Server), the Credit Card Server, Autosequence Server, POS Operations, etc.

In order to reload the database click on the "SQL Database Server" line under the NTSERVER in the left navigation pane (arrow #1 below). Then click on the "Off" radio button. Once the green check mark has turned to a red X, click the "Reload" button.

POS Lifeline.com

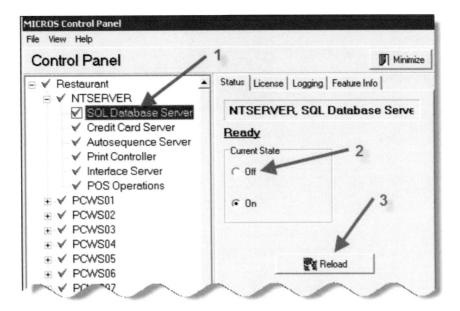

This will reload the database. Follow the same procedures to reload the Credit Card drivers, the Autosequences Drivers, etc.

**Rebooting the System**

It is important that the system be completely rebooted once a week. Open up the Control Panel. Once open, click on the "Restaurant" line at the top of the navigation pane.

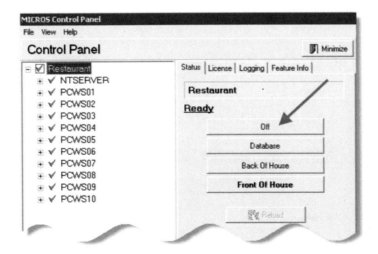

Next, click on the "Off" button. This should turn the entire system off on each terminal and the server itself. When there is a red X next to the "Restaurant" line in the navigation pane move on to the next step. **It is important that the entire restaurant is turned off before continuing.**

Find the Icon on the desktop that looks like this:

Double click on this icon. This will run a command line program in a black box that appears on the screen. It may take a few minutes to go through all of its steps. This program is actually going to each terminal in the restaurant and manually rebooting each and every one of them.

If you do not have this icon on your desktop it is necessary to go to each individual terminal and reboot them manually before continuing on.

Next it is necessary to reboot the server that we are working on.

Click on the Start Menu located in the lower left corner of the screen.

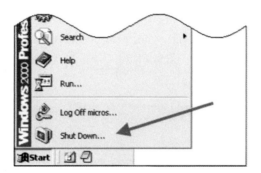

Click on "Shut Down." This will bring up the following window:

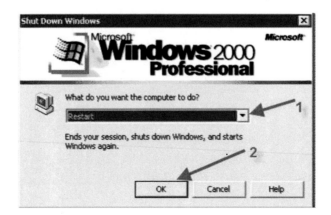

Be sure that the computer is set to "Restart" (arrow #1 above). Then press the "OK" button. This will shut the computer down then restart it.

As the computer restarts it will automatically restart the restaurant program. When the restaurant program has come back up, open up the Control panel and double check to make sure you have all green check marks:

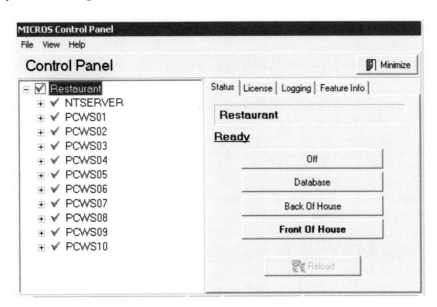

POS Lifeline.com

# POS Configurator

## Introduction

## Overview

The Micros POS system uses a SQL database system that allows it to look up information on a continuous basis and make adjustments to things such as quantity available, price, and clock in status, etc. Without getting bogged down in a long, technical explanation let's just say that all of the terminals talk to each other on a continuous basis. This allows for real time management of product, an accurate system for tracking employee shifts and time card data, and many other functions.

The back office server is the hub of the wheel. Without it the system can function, but it is designed to do the heavy lifting. Especially in a busy environment.

The POS Configurator is a program that simplifies interaction with the database. Through the Configurator we are able to program almost every aspect of the Micros system. We can define where things print, how they look on the screen, hide menu items when they are not available and on and on. Through the Configurator we also manage employee files, grant access to the system and define prices.

Let's start by taking a quick look at the interface. Open up POS Configurator and enter your password. This is the main screen:

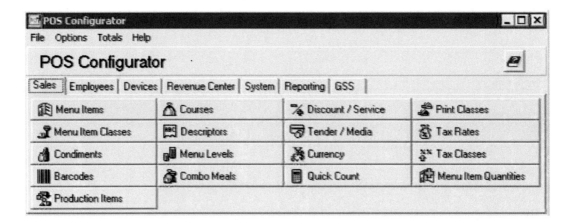

This is the main *Navigation* screen. Utilizing the tabs across the top, "Sales," "Employees," "Devices," "Revenue Center," "System," "Reporting," and, "GSS" we can find the particular part of the database we want to work on or modify.

Notice that items are placed under the appropriate tab. Menu Items, for instance, are placed under the "Sales" tab because these are items that represent sales. Similarly,

"Condiments" are items that modify a Menu Item. So it makes sense that those would be under the Sales tab as well.

It makes sense then, that when working with payroll issues or assigning Jobs that we would find those under the "Employees" tab:

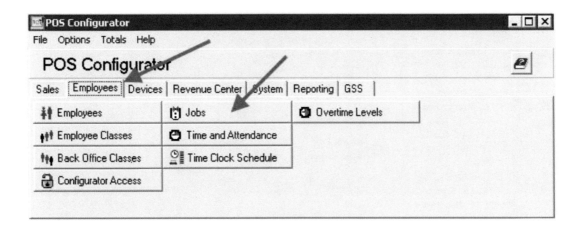

Notice in the screenshot above that the tab that is active has a little box around it. Looking at the shot above we can see that under the Employees tab we can add employees (the employees button), work with Jobs, and set access to various parts of the system.

After using the Navigation screen to find the element we need to work on, click on the appropriate button. For the following example let's go to the "Sales" tab and then click on the "Menu Items" button.

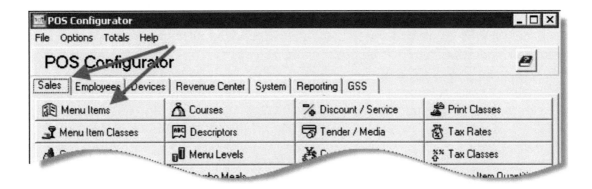

This opens up a section of the POS Configurator that allows us to work on Menu Items.

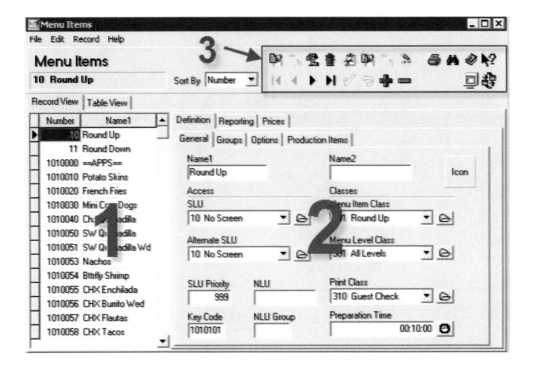

Section 1 is the complete list of every menu item in the database. We call this section the *NAVIGATON AREA*. Using it we can scroll through the database until we find the relevant record to edit.

Section 2 is the *DETAIL AREA*. The detail area shows the detail of the menu item that is highlighted in the Navigation area.

Section 3 is the *TOOLBAR*. The POS Configurator toolbar provides shortcuts to common operations while working anywhere in the Configurator. These shortcuts can save you time as you program or make changes to the database. In addition this is where you can access help that is specific to the task at hand. When you place the mouse pointer over a given icon a description of it will appear on the screen.

Don't worry if you're confused! In all of the following chapters we will go step by step with screenshots to illustrate how to do a given task.

# The *NAVIGATION AREA*

The Navigation Area allows us to find the record that we need to work on.

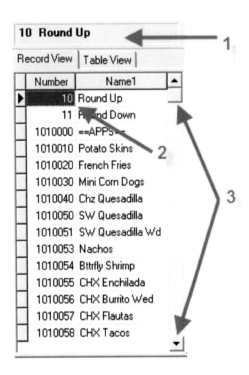

Arrow #1 shows what record is currently selected. Notice that the record is inverted in color (arrow #2). This is another indication that this is the record that is selected. The arrows up and down (arrow #3) allow us to navigate up and down through the database.

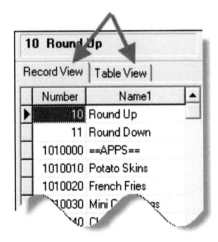

Notice the two tabs at the top of the Navigation area. "Record View" and "Table View" allows for information to be entered into the database two different ways. For the sake of this book, we will work almost exclusively in Record View. Table view is helpful when initially programming a database or making large scale changes to it. It can also be very confusing for new users and is therefore not recommended.

Notice also that each database entry has its own record number. While we will primarily be dealing with the "Name1" of menu items, it can sometimes be very helpful when working with a new menu item or changing an existing one to jot down an item's name and number. When it is helpful to do that you will see a box similar to this:

> **TIP**: You will occasionally see a "Tip" box like this one. Here we try to highlight important, time saving techniques that will speed up a given process or point out some other important bit of information.

## The *DETAIL AREA*

The detail area shows you all of the programmed information for the highlighted record. This is the area where we define how a menu item (record) will behave. When working with Menu Items we define things such as price and the screen that they show up on, etc. When working with Employees we define an employee's name, date of birth, access privileges, etc.

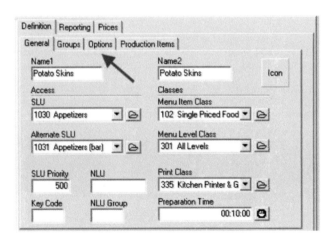

In the example above we are working on the "Potato Skins" menu item. Notice all of the tabs at the top that allow us to define precisely how this item will work within the system. After we define it using the "Definition" tab, we also need to set up its reporting and price information.

We will take a closer look at the various tabs and choices in the chapters that follow.

# The *TOOLBAR*

The Toolbar always floats at the top of the record (or table) screen. It allows us to shorten our keystrokes and do repetitive tasks quickly and easily. Move your cursor over them slowly and a tip will be displayed of their function.

**Cut**

This button removes a record and saves it to the clipboard.

**Copy**

This button copies selected information and saves it to the clipboard without deleting it from the source.

**Paste**

This allows you to paste information from the clipboard into a new location.

**Copy Record**

Use this button to copy an entire record and all of its information to the clipboard. This is an <u>extremely</u> helpful button.

**Paste Record**

Along with the copy record button this allows you to quickly and effortlessly copy records when adding like items.

**Find**

This allows for a quick search for a record that contains a specific value.

**Save Changes**

This button saves any changes you have made to the record and makes them active in the system.

**Undo**

This button reverts the record to the last saved state.

**Insert**

This button inserts a new, blank record at the next available numerical position.

**Delete**

This deletes the current selected record. Note that some records can't be deleted after the have been used to ring in sales or with timekeeping functions.

Help

This brings up the internal help screens for the Micros POS.

Specific Help

Clicking on this button and then on a field gives specific guidance on that field when available. Note that you must click on this button a second time to disengage it before entering data.

Now that we've covered some of the basics, let's go ahead and get started.

# How to Define a New Menu Item

## Adding New Menu Items into the Database

A menu item is any item found on a restaurant menu that is available to the customer for purchase. It is also any item, such as a retail T-Shirt or Hat that isn't on the menu but available for purchase as well. You will also find all condiments and preps in the menu item database.

In the following example we're going to add an import priced bottled beer named "Kalik." Here are the defining factors for our new item:

> Name: Kalik
> Price level: Import
> Type: Bottled Beer
> Visible to: Bar Revenue Center & Café Revenue Center

Let's get started.

Open up the POS Configurator. Select the "Sales" tab then select the "Menu Items" button. Your window should look similar to this:

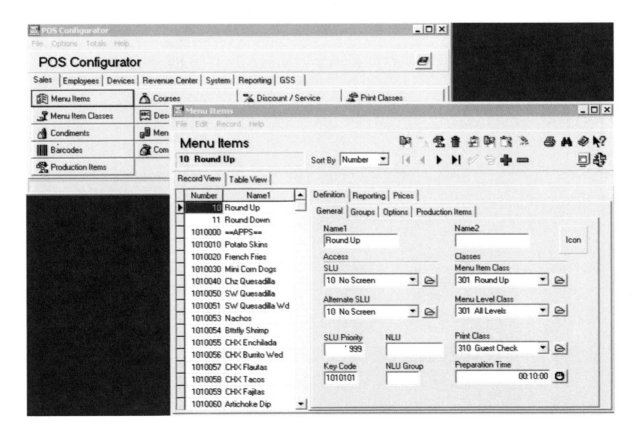

Now we must locate the general group under which the item falls. In this example, we look for the "BEER BOTTLE" group by scrolling down the menu item list until we find it.

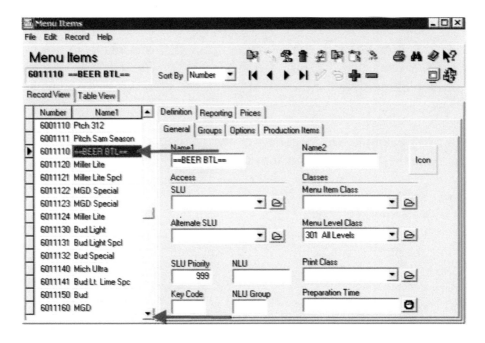

Once we have found the general section (BEER BTL) we can then look for a product that is similar to the one we are adding. In this example we want to find an Import Bottle because our new product, Kalik, is an import.

Locating Corona and clicking on its name brings up the programming information for it in the detail area.

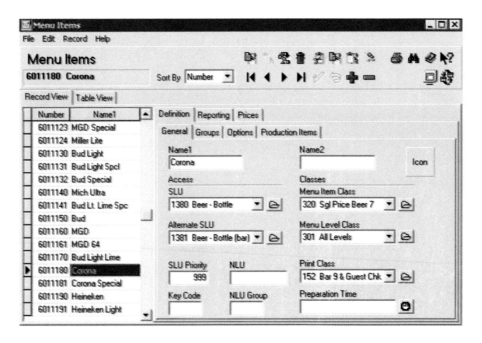

As you can see in the detail area to the right Corona shows up on two screens. The SLU (or Screen Look Up) tells the item where to appear. It shows up on the "Beer – Bottle" screen and it shows up on the "Beer – Bottle (bar)" screen. This is important because the first SLU is in the café revenue center and the second SLU is in the bar revenue center. You can also see that it is defined as a single priced beer and prints to Bar 9 & Guest Check.

> *NOTE*: SLU stands for <u>S</u>creen <u>L</u>ook <u>Up</u>. Each menu item has the ability to show up on any given screen within the POS system. We define which screen it shows up on through the SLU field. If, for instance, we wanted an item to show up on the appetizer screen we would choose that within the SLU field.

It is not important that you know how all of this works at this time. Because this item is going to be identical to the one we are adding, we are going to simply copy this menu item record and then change the name for our new product.

With the name highlighted go to the Edit Menu and click on the "Copy Record" option:

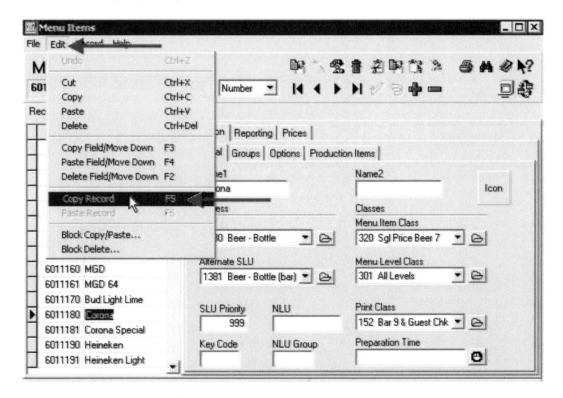

Now go back to the Edit Menu and select the "Paste Record" option. The database will add a record in the next available location. In this example it becomes item 6011182. Notice that you now have two items named "Corona."

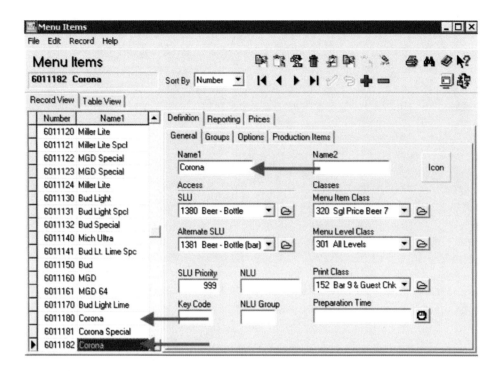

Now change the name of the new item in the "Name 1" field in the definition area to the right of the product list (where the top red arrow is above) and click on the green check to save it.

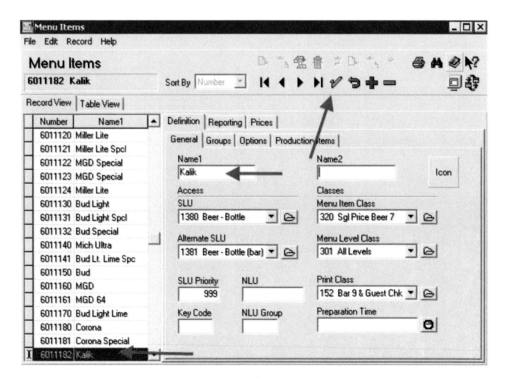

One last thing we'll want to do is to check to make sure the price is correct. In the middle of the detail window is a tab marked, "Prices." Click on this tab and verify that the price

is correct. If necessary, change the price and again click on the green check mark to save the item.

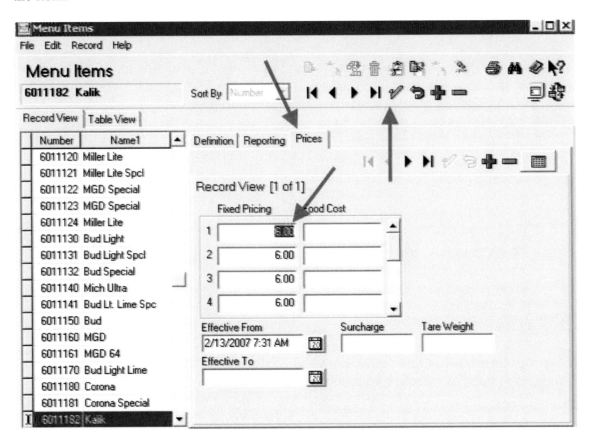

Congratulations! You've just added a new menu item!

# How to Define a New Food Menu Item

## Adding New Menu Items into the Database

A menu item is any item found on a restaurant menu that is available to the customer for purchase. It is also any item, such as a retail T-Shirt or Hat that isn't on the menu but available for purchase as well. A food menu item differs from a bar item in that there are usually multiple modifiers that need to be defined when a server is placing an order.

In the following exercise we're going to add a dinner item to the "Specials" menu. Here are the defining factors for our new item:

> Name: Sautéed Grouper
> Price: $ 28.95
> Type: "Specials" Item
> Add on sides: 2 to be entered by the server
> Food preparation: Not needed because we know it's sautéed

Let's get started.

Open up the POS Configurator. Select the "Sales" tab then select the "Menu Items" button. Your window should look similar to this:

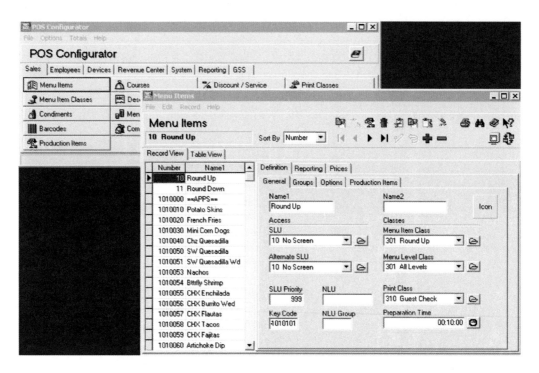

Now we must locate the general group under which the item falls. In this example, we look for the "SPECIALS" group by scrolling down the menu item list until we find it.

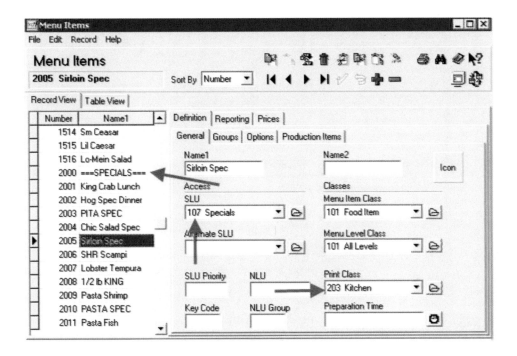

Once we have found the general section (===SPECIALS===) we can then look for a product that is similar to the one we are adding. In this example we want to find a special that is active (meaning that it is currently showing up on the SPECIALS SLU). In the picture above the "Sirloin Spec" is highlighted. Looking to the right we can see that it shows up on the "Specials" SLU meaning that it is active. (For an in depth discussion of making items active and inactive, please see the manual, "Making Menu Items Active / Inactive").

In addition you can see that it prints to the Kitchen (as defined by the print class).

Because the item we are adding is going to be similar to the one we have highlighted, "Sirloin Spec" we are simply going to copy and paste this menu item record and then change a few things to make it what we want.

With the name highlighted go to the Edit Menu and click on the "Copy Record" option:

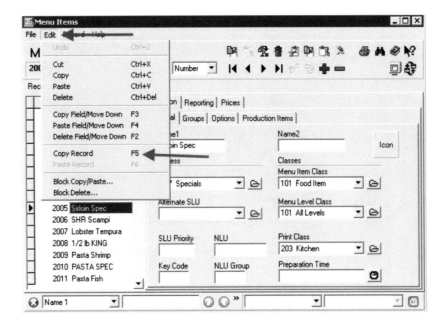

Now go back to the Edit Menu and select the "Paste Record" option. The database will add a record in the next available location. In this example it becomes item 2207. Note that you now have two items named "Sirloin Spec."

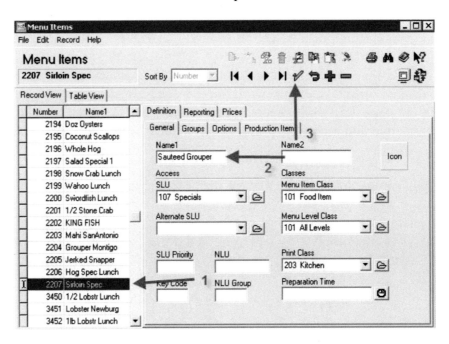

The red arrow marked #1 above points out the current item we are working on. Now change the name of the new item in the "Name 1" field in the definition area to the right of the menu item list (where the red arrow marked #2 is above) and click on the green check to save it. This is how it will look when you have finished:

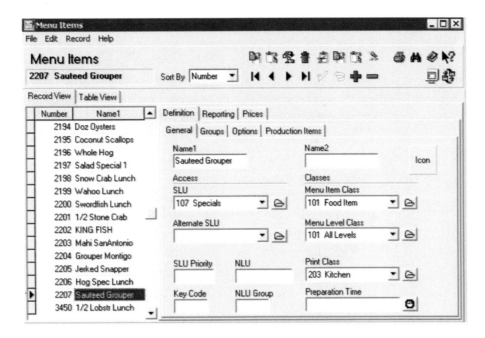

The next thing we'll want to do is make sure that the item prompts for the required modifiers (such as how to prepare, temperature to cook, the appropriate number of sides, etc).

Looking at the image below, follow the first red arrow marked with a "1". Click on the tab marked, "Groups."

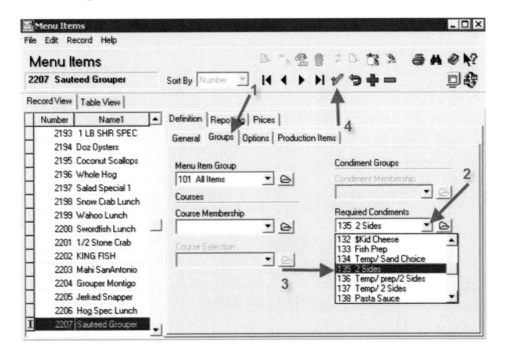

Looking at the arrow marked "2" shows you the "Required Condiments" that will come up for the server when they choose this item from the menu. In this example we need to

set it to prompt for 2 side choices but not a temperature or preparation. (We know that it is sautéed already).

Press on the down arrow (arrow #2) and a drop down box will appear allowing us to chose the correct "Required Condiments." Once selected (arrow #3) go up and save by clicking on the green check mark (arrow #4 in the image above).

Finally, the last thing we'll want to do is to put the correct price in.

> *TIP:* Many restaurants use multiple price levels because they run a happy hour special or similar promotion on food. Therefore it is necessary to fill out each price level field with the correct information. Failure to do this can lead to incorrect pricing or no price at all.

In the middle of the detail window is a tab marked "Prices." Click on this tab and enter the correct price. If necessary, change all of the price fields to reflect the new price and then click on the green check mark to save the item.

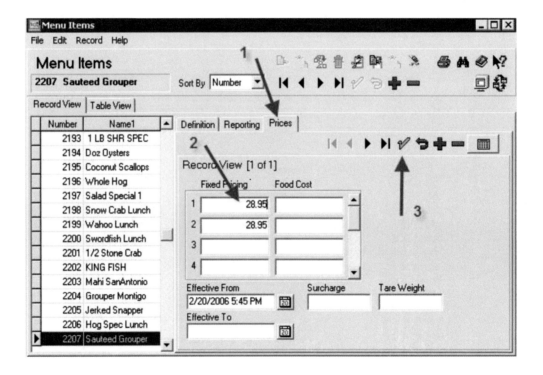

Congratulations! You've just added a new menu item! When the server presses the "Sautéed Grouper" button it will prompt for 2 sides and then send the order to the kitchen.

# Making Menu Items Active / Inactive

## Using the Find / Search Function

Menu items are the heart of the POS system. They enable us to charge for items on the menu, retail goods in the store, apply condiments and a host of other functions.

With many restaurants running daily specials in both the bar and restaurant (the bar revenue center and the restaurant revenue center), it is often necessary to create new menu item buttons on an ongoing basis. The result of creating new buttons is that a system often becomes overloaded with buttons that are not actually being used.

For example: The Chef runs a "Jerked Snapper" entrée on Monday night but not on Tuesday. On Monday he or one of the Managers creates a button named, "Jerked Snapper" that shows up under the "Specials" menu screen. On Tuesday, that key is still there but the special has already sold out and is no longer available. Now take this example and multiply it by two weeks. If the Chef has one different special every day for 14 days, the "Specials" menu screen is now crowded with 14 keys that are not being used! Imagine a new server trying to order the correct item – how long would it take them to find it? What effect on the customer's dining experience would this have?

So how do we clean it all up? Simple! We make the non-used items "*inactive.*" Why make them "*inactive*" rather than just change the names to something else? We do this for reporting purposes. The following week, month, or year, the Chef or Owner might want to know how a particular item sold. By making an item "*inactive*" we keep it and its sales history in the POS system for future reference.

The purpose of this exercise is to work through how we can "activate" and "de-activate" buttons that appear under the order screens in order to maintain a system that is efficient. This in turn will streamline the servers so they have more time to engage with the customers and turn tables more quickly.

In the following exercise we will:

1. Use the "Find" function to look for a specific menu item (Jerked Snapper)
2. Activate & De-Activate a particular menu item

POS Lifeline.com

## Using the FIND Function

First we'll need to get logged into the POS Configurator. Once there, select the "Sales" tab, and then select the "Menu Items" button. Your window should look similar to this:

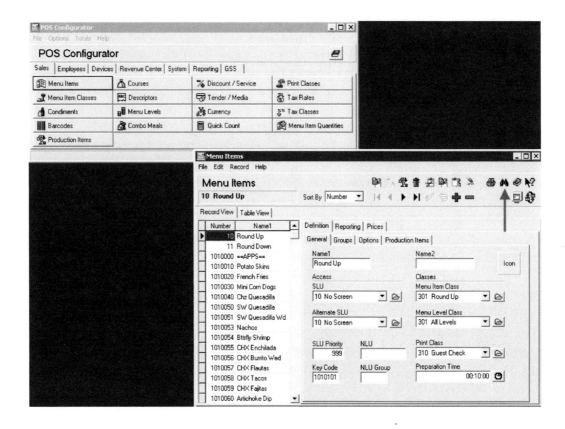

Across the top of the Menu Items window on the right side there is a picture of binoculars. This icon is the "Search / Find" button. The red arrow in the image above points to it. Press that button.

The window has expanded, showing additional choices on the bottom. In the image below there are four red arrows. Beginning with the first arrow on the left, this box tells the computer which field to search in. In this case it is going to look in the "Name 1" field. The second box is the "Search Box" where we type in the "Name 1" that we're looking for. The orange triangles directly to the right of the box tell the computer which direction to look in – either up the database or down.

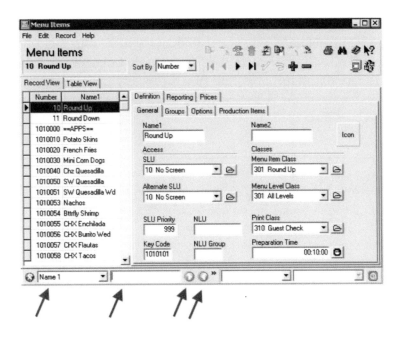

So let's go ahead and fill in the "Search Box" with the name we're trying to find: "Snapper"

---

**TIP**: Sometimes it is difficult to remember what the exact spelling of a menu item was. In that case, simply put in the most logical combination of letters that might bring it up. If we're trying to find "Jerked Snapper", we might search for just "Snapper" and see what comes up.

---

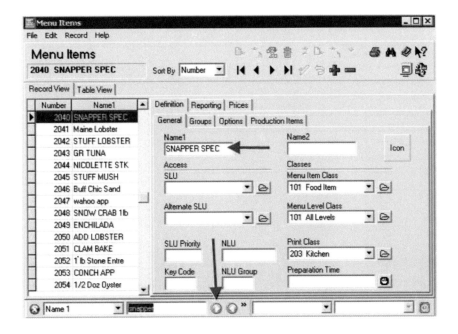

Once you've entered the name, press on the first arrow key to the right of the box to look down the database. This will take us to the first item that matches our criteria. Since this is not the item we're looking for, press the first arrow key to the right of the box again to look further down the database. This will take us to the next entry. Continue doing this until the correct item is displayed.

> **TIP**: "I know that the item is there but when I search down, I can't find it." When this happens, use the triangle button to the right. This will look through the database in the opposite direction.

Once the menu item has been located we can move onto the next step of activating or de-activating it.

### Activating and De-Activating a Menu Item

In the image below we are looking at the programming information for the menu item "Jerked Snapper." Changing the SLU (Screen Look Up) for the item changes where in the system the item will show up. In this case, it is currently programmed to show up on the "Specials" screen.

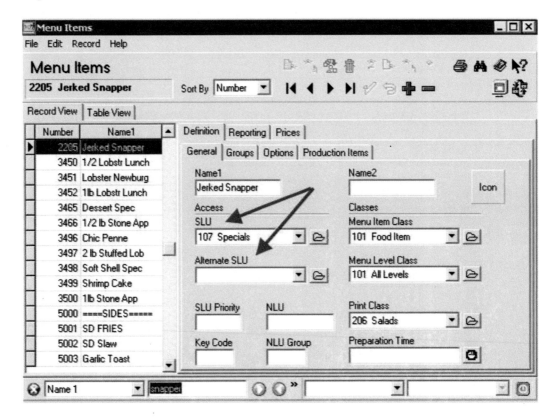

To make the item inactive, we simply click in the SLU box and press the DELETE Key. This will make the box blank meaning that the menu item will no longer show up on any screens. Be sure to then click on the green check mark in order to save the changes you've made. The menu item is still in the system, but now it's *inactive*.

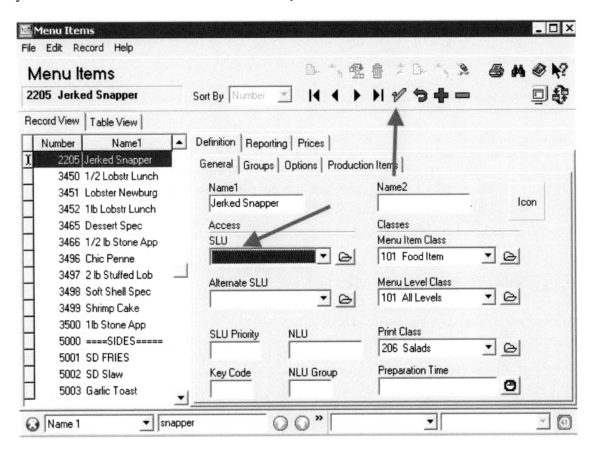

Likewise, if we wanted to make an item active, we would change the SLU from blank to the appropriate screen.

Thats all there is to it! With just a little effort the manager can keep menus well maintained, the servers happy and the focus on customer service where it belongs.

Once you're done with the menu items go ahead and close out of the POS Configurator.

# Working With Prices

## One Time Price Changes & Ongoing Specials

In this section we'll work with the ways Micros handles price records. When we're finished we'll be able to do a one time price change, set up the POS to run a special price for a menu item once a week and run a once a month price special.

In the following exercise we will cover the following:

> Identify which day is "day 1" in the system
> Enter a static price for a menu item
> Enter a once a week discount price for an item
> Change an item's Menu Class to look for the additional price records
> Enter a once a month discount price for an item
> Add price records

### Identifying "Day 1" in the Micros System

Micros uses "Day x" to identify which prices should be active on any given day. For instance Day 1 might be set up as a Monday. Thus Day 2 would be Tuesday, etc. As we move forward to program our specials for a given day we must first identify the way the system is set up.

Open up POS Configurator and go to the Sales tab. Now click on the Menu Levels tab.

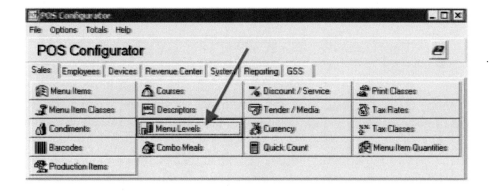

When the "Menu Levels" dialogue box comes up, click on the "Auto Menu Levels" tab (arrow #1 below).

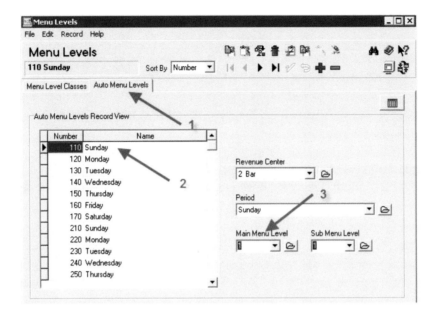

Note that Sunday (arrow #2) is highlighted in the navigation section of the window. In the detail section to the right is the programmed information for Sunday. Arrow #3 shows us that Sunday is "Main Menu Level" number 1. This indicates that the system is set up so that Sunday is "Day 1 / Price 1." You'll see how this affects our programming of specials shortly. Jot this information down on a sheet of scratch paper for reference later.

You can now close the window "Menu Levels."

## Entering a Static Price for a Menu Item

In the following example we need to add a price to a bottle of beer named "Bell's Beer." After locating the item in the database, click on the "Prices Tab" (arrow #1) for the menu item.

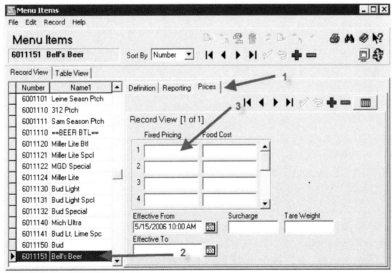

Note in the screen shot above that we know we're looking at Bell's Beer because that is the record that is highlighted in the navigation portion of the widow (arrow #2). After clicking on the "Prices" tab we see that there is a field called "Fixed Pricing" (arrow #3). This is where we'll enter the price for the beer. Note that the fields are numbered starting with #1.

Because we are adding a static price, or a price that won't change, we need only to fill out the first price field (Fixed Price #1). The system will default to that price when no others are set.

> **TIP**: If your system is programmed with a Happy Hour, it will be necessary to enter a price for fields 1 & 2. If you're system has been programmed for multiple price levels throughout the course of a day or week it may be necessary to enter more than 2 price fields.

Let's go ahead and enter a price of $5.00 in field 1 and save it using the green check mark. Once we're done it should look like this:

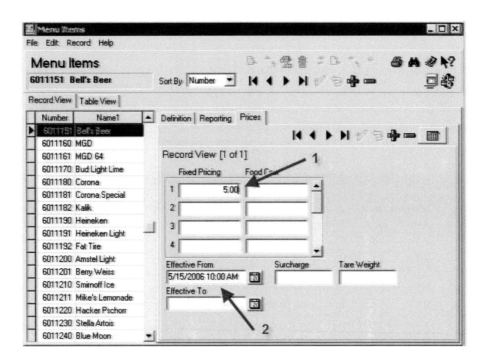

Note the box near the bottom (arrow #2). The "Effective From" "Effective To" boxes allow us to set up start and end times for our pricing. When setting up static prices, just be sure the "Effective From" box is filled in with the date you program the menu item.

POS Lifeline.com

Leaving the "Effective To" box empty tells the system that this is an ongoing or default price for the menu item.

## Enter a once a week discount price for an item

Now that we're familiar with the price record, lets make our "Bell's Beer" menu item reflect a once a week special price of $3.00 on Wednesdays.

When an item has more than one price we call it a "Multi-Priced Item." When changing an item from a single price to a multiple priced item we must do two things. The first is to program prices for each day. The second is to change its Menu Item Class.

> **TIP**: Menu Item Classes are used to apply a set of options and properties to a group of menu items. In this example by using the Menu Item Class we can tell the system to look for a different price everyday.

Open up the POS Configurator and locate the Bell's Beer menu item in the database. Once located, go to the "Prices" tab. Remember how we only filled out "Fixed Pricing" field 1 before? Now we are going to work with the other "Fixed Pricing" fields to give us a special price on Wednesday of $3.00.

Earlier we discovered that the system identifies "Day 1" with Sunday. That makes Wednesday day 4. Therefore we need to change this item into a Multiple Priced Menu Item (it will have more than one price during the week – we will do this in the next section) and give it a price for each of the seven days.

Moving down the "Fixed Pricing" fields, fill in the correct price for each of the seven days. Remember that Wednesday, Day 4, should be priced at $3.00.

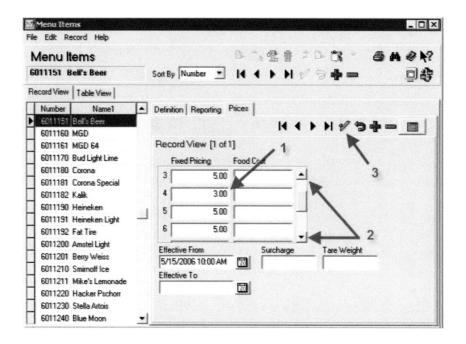

Notice that we've added prices for all seven days, with Day 4 being the special price of $3.00 (arrow #1). We can scroll through the different prices using the up and down arrow keys to the right (arrow #2). Don't forget to save your changes (arrow #3)!

## Change an Item's Menu Class to Look for the Additional Price Records

Now that we've given this menu item multiple prices, we'll need to do one last thing. That's to let the system know to look for more than one price. Click on the "Definition" tab then the "General Tab."

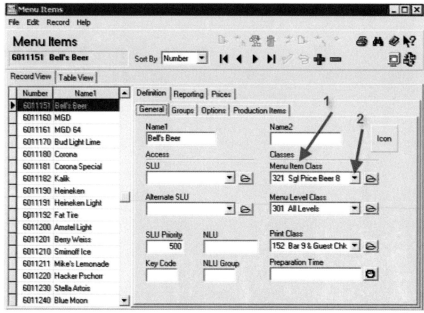

To the right is a field for "Menu Item Class." You can see that it currently is set as a "Sgl Price Beer" signifying that the POS system only sees one price for it (arrow #1). We'll need to change this to a multiple priced beer. Click on the arrow to the right of the "Menu Item Class" field (arrow #2). A drop down box will appear allowing you to choose the correct class. Look for a "Mul Price Beer" choice and select it. This tells the system that the prices change from day to day.

Don't forget to save the menu item changes!

## Enter a once a month discount price for an item

In the following example, we will program an item - we'll stick with Bell's Beer - to be a special promotional price one day a month. You might need this type of special if a distributor sponsored a monthly promotion at your establishment. In the following example, we'll set the POS to charge just $1.00 for a Bell's Beer on the first Monday of each month.

In the previous examples, we changed different "Fixed Pricing" fields to reflect the day of the week. We did this within one "Pricing Record." Micros allows us to set up multiple pricing records for each menu item for specific events or time frames. Each Price Record has the same number of available "Fixed Pricing" fields that we can work with. This allows us to single out a specific day of the year for a unique price structure. Confused? Don't worry! We'll go through it step by step!

Let's go back and locate our "Bell's Beer" menu item. Once it comes up, go to the "Price" tab.

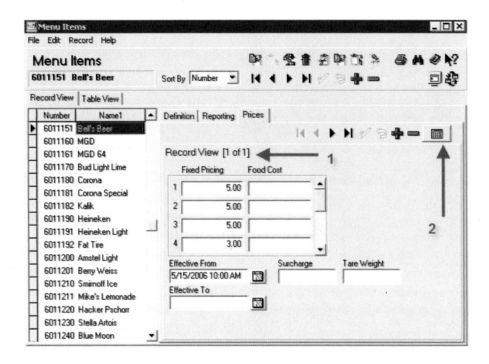

Note that arrow #1 shows us that we are looking at "Record #1" in the record view format. Notice that for this record we have multiple prices (in the "Fixed Pricing" fields). Press the button to the right that looks similar to a list (arrow #2). This will give you the following display:

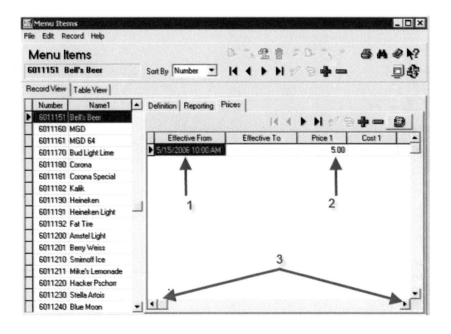

This display shows you the different "Price Records" all at the same time. Rather than read from top to bottom, like the Record View we were looking at, they now read left to right. We can see that the record we set up earlier is the only one that exists for this menu item (arrow #1). If we use the scroll buttons (arrow #3) we can move to the right and see how our prices change on day 4 (Wednesday) for our special.

We're happy with our pricing during the week but want to enter in the pricing specials for the one day a month that Bell's Beer will be sold for $1.00. In order to have the system automatically change the pricing for just those days, we will need to create a new price record for each of those days. Since there will be 12 such days, we will need to make 12 new price records.

**Adding Price Records**

Using the "Insert Price" icon (the arrow below) will allow us to add a new record. Click on that button once.

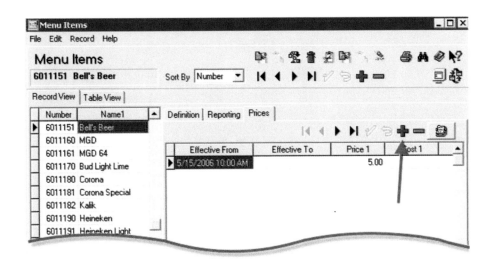

The POS puts a new price record below the existing one. Click inside this blue box and the following will show up:

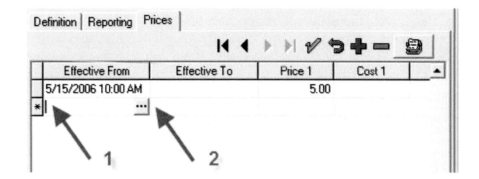

Notice that the cursor is now in the "Effective From" field and there is a box with an ellipsis in it. Click on the box with the ellipsis. This will bring up a calendar. This is the easiest way to define when we want this new price record to take effect. For the sake of our exercise, we will enter January 5, 2009 (the first Monday in January). We want the price to take effect before we open for business. So let's go ahead and set it for 9 am.

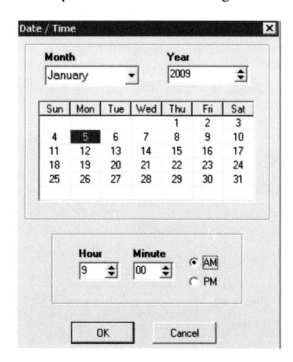

When you've got it set correctly click on OK. Do the same for the "Effective To" field, this time setting it to be effective until sometime after the business closes. This will ensure the price will be active for only the date specified. Finally, enter our $1.00 price in the "Price 2" field to the right. We use "Price 2" because the menu item is set up as a multiple priced item. Therefore on Mondays it will be looking for Price 2. Be careful to enter the price on the correct price record line. It should look like this:

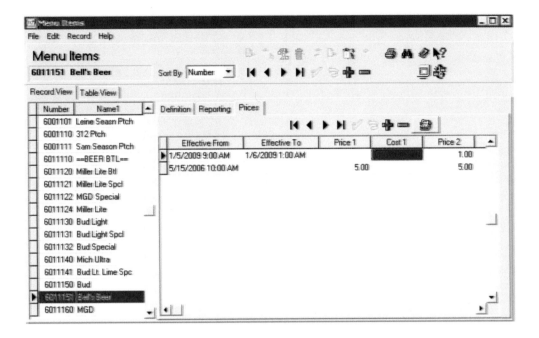

Now go ahead and save it. If you watched closely you noticed that the price record you just added switched places with the record that was already there. This indicates that the record that doesn't have an "Effective To" field filled in is the default price record.

Continue to add new price records as needed for this menu item. In our example, when we're done it looks like this:

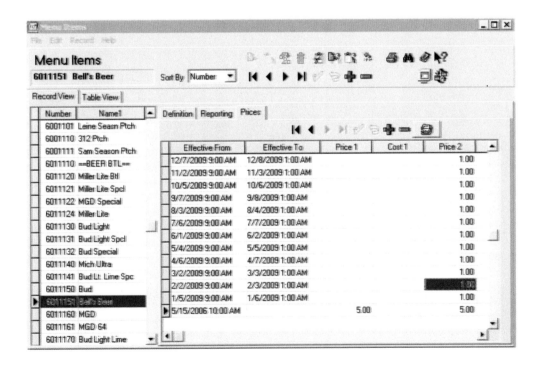

Notice that for each special event we added a record that would essentially "turn on" for the day and then "turn off" once the day had passed.

Once you've finished, be certain to Save using the green check mark.

# Working with Condiments

## Required Condiments

Condiments are modifiers that an employee adds when ordering a menu item. It allows the wait staff to communicate the choices of the customer to both the kitchen and the bar. Examples of a condiment include "medium rare," "with mayonnaise" and "on the rocks." A server can only enter condiments after a main menu item has been selected (such as an entrée). Condiments modify the main menu item. Condiments are entered into the database through POS Configurator as a type of Menu Item. While one of the more confusing aspects of the POS system, being able to programming it is probably one of the most important.

> **NOTE**: The terms "condiment" and "modifier" are interchangeable. Micros uses the term Condiment within POS Configurator for programming purposes. Condiments modify (hence they are a 'modifier') a menu item and can only be applied after a menu item has been chosen.

Consider the following example. In a busy restaurant where there are 5 servers the Chef has added one new special. The special requires a preparation temperature and the choice of two sides (3 condiments). The Chef and the manager are not familiar with how to make the system prompt for these three modifiers. Therefore when any of the 5 servers order this special the Chef or someone from the line must track down the server in order to find out what those three choices are. Those three choices must then be audibled over a busy line to the kitchen. In short this is a recipe for disaster. Customer satisfaction is certain to be compromised and wasted product can be expected.

Required Condiments are condiments that the server must enter before the system will place the order to the kitchen or the bar. This section will walk the reader through setting up a new condiment choice from start to finish.

> **NOTE**: This section assumes that the POS system for the business has been initially set up and running. If that is not the case then a more in-depth review of menu item classes and reporting classes is in order and a professional should be brought in to handle this more complicated programming. If you have been operational for any amount of time it is usually acceptable to assume that the fundamentals have already been programmed in the system. If that initial programming has not been satisfactorily done, we will discover that in the first section, "Step 1: Enter and Define the Condiments in the Menu Item Section."

## Getting Started – An Overview

To effectively utilize condiments it is recommended that some preliminary planning be done. Ask yourself the following questions:

1. Which condiments does this new menu item need?
2. Are those condiments already in the system?
3. Will these condiments add or subtract $ value to the menu item?
4. Will I need to track these condiments in the system?

### Condiment Groups

Think of condiment groups as a subset of all of the available condiments that are in the system. If the entire list of condiments (or modifiers) includes everything from what juice a vodka drink should have to the preparation of a fish dish then a subset might be condiments that modify a beverage. Utilizing condiment groups allows us to narrow down the modifiers we want to appear on the screen for the server when a regular menu item is ordered.

For example: let's suppose we're working on a beef entrée that comes with one side. We would probably want 3 condiment groups to come up, one after the other, that allow us to define our entrée for the kitchen.

The first group would be one that asks the server for the preparation temperature. We might have 5 condiments (modifiers) that belong to this group: Rare, Medium Rare, Medium, Medium Well and Well.

The second condiment group that we would want is a choice of side for the entrée. This group might be comprised of 4 choices: Green Beans, Broccoli, Rice and Potato.

Finally the third group we want to come up is a more general one where the server can communicate with the kitchen. This group could have many condiments in it such as: Allergy, No Sauce, Split Plate, etc.

> **NOTE**: The Micros POS allows for up to 256 different condiment groups. In addition condiments may be assigned to different groups. Membership is not limited to any one group. The modifier (condiment) "SEE SERVER" for instance might be a member of all groups.

Condiment groups therefore allow us to focus on particular condiments that work well with the entree in a process that flows naturally. Servers can work through their orders in a natural progression similar to how they take an order tableside.

## The Programming Process

In order to program condiments we will step through the following process:

1.  Enter and define the condiments in the Menu Item section
2.  Create and define the Condiment Groups
3.  Create and define Condiment Membership
4.  Create and define Condiment Selection
5.  Connect the Condiment Menu Items to the Condiment Membership
6.  Enter and define our new Menu Item in the POS System
7.  Connect the Condiment Selection to the Menu Item

In the following walk through we will be programming a condiment group that will prompt for a fish preparation and a choice of side. The restaurant in question has never sold fish before and will therefore need to have all fish preparation condiments (modifiers) added to the system. The sides are already programmed into the system. We will also need to add a menu item for the fish (Snapper will be our example) and link it to the condiments (modifiers) we have programmed. Let's get started!

## Step 1: Enter and Define the Condiments in the Menu Item Section

### Step 1a: Prepare to Program

In order to get started we need to define what condiments we need to program. The best way to do this is write them out and then run them through the questions we asked ourselves at the outset in the Overview section.

1.  Which condiments does this new menu item need?
    We know we need to define how the fish is cooked. For our example it will be:
    Blackened
    Grilled
    Fried

2.  Are those condiments already in the system?
    No. Because this is the first time that fish has been added we will need to create these condiments (modifiers) from scratch.

3.  Will these condiments add or subtract $ value to the menu item?
    These condiments will not add or subtract value from the menu item.

4.  Will I need to track these condiments in the system?
    No. Because these condiments (modifiers) are merely a preparation, they do not need to be tracked by the database so that they show up on a report.

Based upon the answers to our questions we now know that we need to create 3 new condiment menu items and then create a condiment group, which we will call "Fish Prep" that will pull these three choices from the hundreds of condiments available.

> **TIP**: For a detailed explanation of how to navigate through the database and how to use the "FIND" function please see the section titled, "POS Configurator," and, "Making Items Active / Inactive" respectively.

**Step 1b: Create a New Section Header in the Database**

Open up POS Configurator then the Sales Tab and then Menu Items. Look for a section of the database similar to "==REQD MODS==". Notice that even within in the POS Configurator the term Modifier and Condiment is interchangeable.

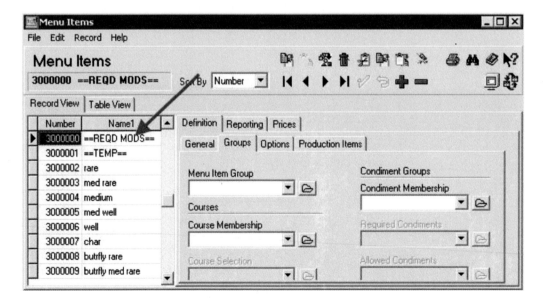

In our example above notice that the "==REQD MODS==" and "==TEMP==" are headers for that section of the database. These are helpful guides that are placed throughout the database to break up the overall database into smaller more manageable sections. They are not necessary and might not have been added to your database at the time of installation. Don't worry if they're not there. Simply look for something that is similar to what we are working on. In this example it would be "rare" or "medium rare" etc. As a meat prep it is very similar to the fish prep options that we are going to add.

> *NOTE*: If you are adding condiments / modifiers to the general section – such as to "Mod A" (for 'A' Modifiers) you can skip this section. This is added into the workflow in order to make the database more organized and is not necessary for Condiments to work correctly.

In our example database above we are going to find the bottom of the meat prep choices and add our new section.

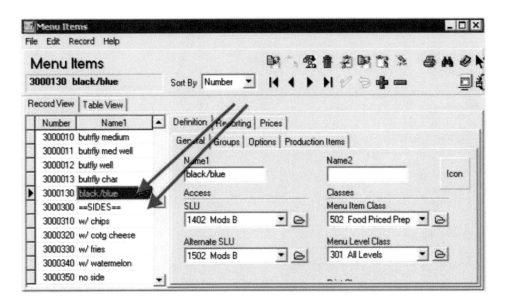

Notice that the record 3000130 "black/blue" is the last of the prep choices and then it skips to 3000300 "==SIDES==". This makes a perfect place for us to add a header for "==FISH PREP==" and our condiments of Blackened, Grilled or Fried.

With the "black/blue" record highlighted, click on the ➕ key to add a new record. This will add a record in the next available slot (number 3000131) that is blank.

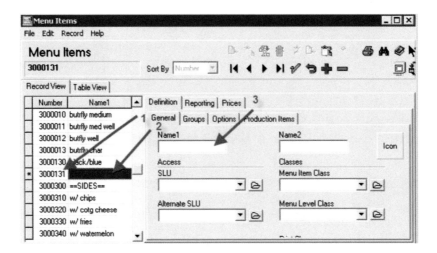

Arrow #1 shows the new record number, arrow 2 the blank name field, and arrow 3 where we are going to define this as a placeholder or header. In the name field enter, "==FISH PREP==". Because this is merely a header or placeholder, we need only to make sure all of the relevant fields in the DETAIL AREA are clear:

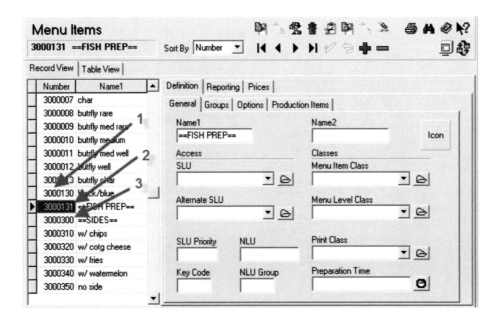

Looking closely at the record numbers it becomes obvious that between the last meat prep (record number 3000130) and the following section "==SIDES==" (record number 3000300) there is room for 170 records! In an effort to keep the database neat and organized then, we will renumber our "==FISH PREP==" record to 3000175. After you have renumbered it and save it, it will look like this:

POS Lifeline.com

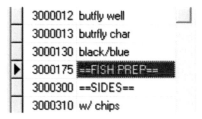

That will allow us to enter more meat preps should the need arise down the road and helps keep the database organized for when we are trying to troubleshoot problems, etc.

**Step 1c: Create and Define a New Condiment (Modifier)**

OK. This is where we're going to add our three new condiments (modifiers): Blackened, Grilled and Fried.

Highlight the "==FISH PREP==" record and click on the ✚ button to add a new record. Then add the name "Blackened" to the Name 1 field in the detail area.

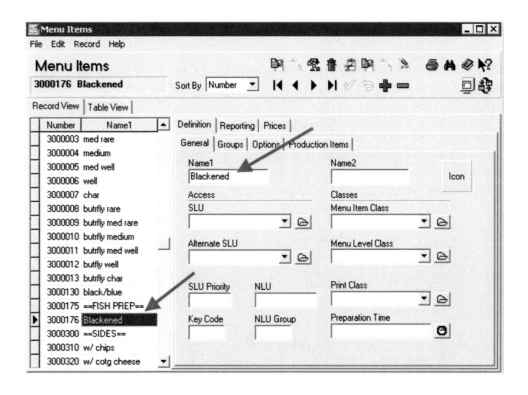

The next step is to fill out the relevant fields in the detail area. For this example we want the modifier to show up under the "B Modifiers" menu screens. In this particular restaurant there are two revenue centers – the bar and the café. So we need to define the SLU screens as both the bar and café.

## Step 1d: Defining a Non-Priced Preparation Condiment

Almost all condiments / modifiers will not add or subtract value from the Menu Item. We will cover both ways of programming however.

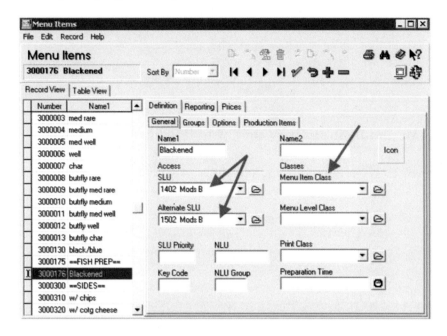

The next step is to define the Menu Item Class. Using the drop down arrow next to the Menu Item Class (arrow #1) scroll through the options until you find ***PREP CLASSES***. This is where we will define how the condiment behaves. In our example we are looking for a *Food Prep* class that does not include price (arrow #2).

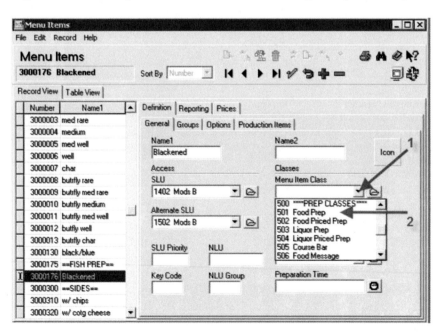

Click on "Food Prep" and save using the green check mark.

## Step 1e: Defining a Priced Preparation Condiment

If, however, you want the condiment / modifier to charge (or discount) the bill you would choose the *Food Priced Prep* Menu Item Class at this stage. In order to charge a price then you would need to enter one in the price record (arrow #1 below) in the DETAIL AREA. Don't forget to enter an "Effective From" date and save it.

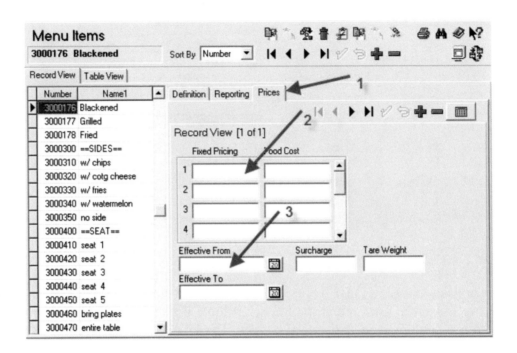

NOTE: If the Menu Item Class drop down box does NOT have a ***PREP CLASSES*** option, including a FOOD PREP choice, your system will require additional programming of Menu Item Classes. At this point you should contact an outside source to properly set up the system.

**Step 1f: Defining the Menu Level Class and Print Class**

Next, move down the detail area and click on the drop down arrow next to the Menu Level Class. The restaurant is going to be running these Modifiers at all times so find "All Levels" and click on that.

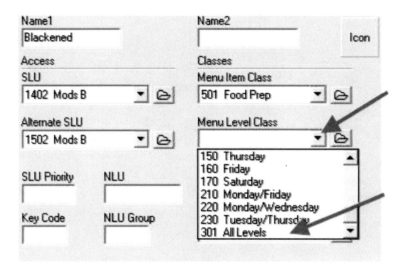

Next is the Print Class. Because this is a food condiment (modifier) that will print in the kitchen, we want it to print red at the kitchen remote printer. This will be easier for the kitchen to read and distinguish between entrees. The Print Class that we're looking for is called, "Food Preps (RED)."

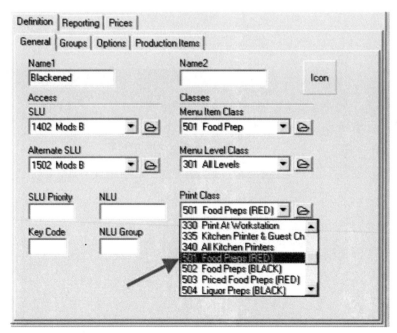

> **TIP**: One final setting on the Definition | General tab that can be set is the SLU priority. This setting from 1 to 999 is useful when you want the choices to come up in an order other than alphabetical. If you were to set Fried to 100 and Blackened to 200, for instance, Fried would appear higher up in the list than Blackened.

## Step 1g: Defining the Condiment Membership Group

Next go to the Definition | Group tab (arrows #1 & 2). The Condiment Membership (arrow #3) is where we will define what group this new modifier belongs to. But we will have to come back to this screen because we haven't yet created a group called, "Fish Prep."

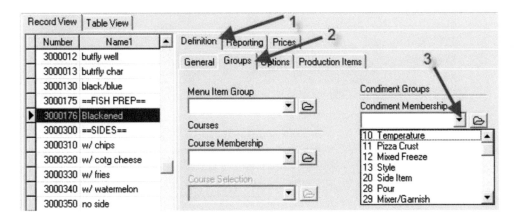

## Step 1h: Defining the Reporting Group

Next go to the Reporting tab in the DETAIL AREA. This can be set up for the system to track the sales numbers for this condiment.

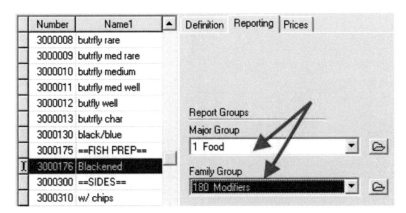

Once you've completed the Report Groups you're done with this condiment for the time being. We will need to come back to it and define condiment membership. Now that the condiment has been defined the easiest way to create the other two condiments is to copy and paste the record and make the minor adjustments to the Name 1 fields and the SLU.

Once complete you should have 3 condiments entered into the POS system that looks like this:

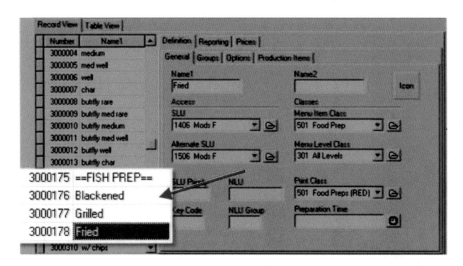

> **TIP**: Now that the three condiments are in the system, take a minute and jot down the record numbers. This will help make it easier when we are trying to find them later.

## Step 2: Create and Define the Condiment Groups

Open up the Sales tab in POS Configurator. Then click on the Condiments button:

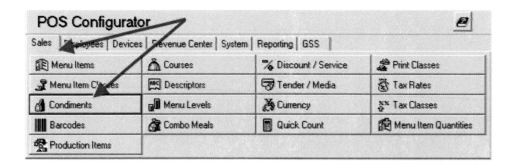

This will bring up the Condiment dialogue box:

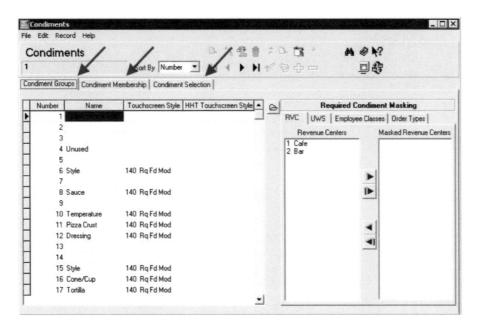

Notice the three tabs across the top. This is where we will define how the condiments work within the system. The first tab, "Condiment Groups" is our first stop. This is where we will create the small group known as "Fish Prep."

> *TIP*: Think of the condiment picture as a line that starts at the Condiment Menu Item (the one we entered in the menu items area) then connects to Condiment Membership, which then connects to the Condiment Group which then connects to the Condiment Selection which then connects to the Menu Item (the entrée). All of these steps are necessary before Condiments will work properly.

## Step 2b: Defining the Condiment Group

The condiment group is the smallest sub-set of condiments. We will be linking our condiments that we just added to only one group so it is important that we keep it as small as possible. For the purpose of this exercise we will create a "Fish Prep" group that will have only the fish prep modifiers in it. Even though we will need to add a "Side Dish" later we will not include those modifiers in this prep group.

Open up the Configurator | Sales | Condiments. Next click on the Condiment Groups tab (arrow #1). Highlight one of blank "Name" fields in the Condiment Group tab. We'll be working with number 2 (arrow #2). Click in the box and add the name, "Fish Prep."

POS Lifeline.com

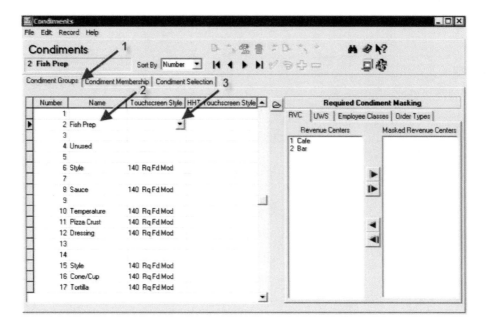

Next go directly to the right to the Touchscreen style. You'll notice that this field has a drop down arrow. Click on the arrow and look for the appropriate Touchscreen style.

> *TIP*: The Touchscreen Style defines how the modifier buttons will show up on the screen for the employees. Arrangement elements such as right to left or up and down, color, button size, etc. This field must be defined. For continuity you'll want to use whatever the other condiment groups are set up to use.

Find "RqFd Mod." This stands for Required Food Modifiers. Looking at the example above you'll notice that the Touchscreen style for all of the other modifiers is "140 RqFd Mod." For continuity let's stick with that one for our new condiments.

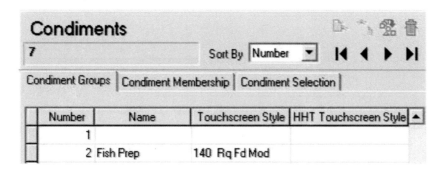

The HHT Touchscreen style refers to Hand Held Touchscreen Style. If your operation uses handhelds enter the style that is used for the other modifier groups lower on the list.

We know that we want the POS system to prompt for fish prep and also a choice of side. So while were here let's make sure that the modifier group for "Side Item" exists. Scroll down the list until you find the condiment group.

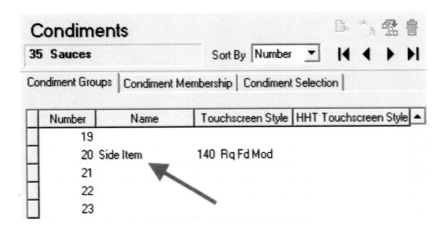

Now that we know for sure that it has been programmed we can move on to the next step.


**Step 2c: Defining Condiment Membership**

Go to the Condiment Membership tab.

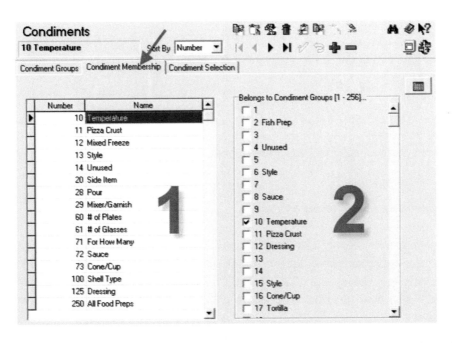

Condiment Membership is how we link our condiment (the one we entered into the Menu Item list) to the condiment group.

The area to the left (#1) is where we tell the POS System to link to the condiments we programmed earlier. The area on the right (#2) is where we link to the Condiment Group. In area #2 you can see that our Condiment Group for "Fish Prep" shows up as number 2. We must therefore create a Membership for the Condiment Menu Item to find it.

> *TIP*: This is the most confusing element of Condiment Programming. If you stay with the step-by-step instructions you'll do just fine! Think of Condiment Membership as the link between the Condiment Menu Item and the Condiment Group.

Click the ➕ button to add a new record. POS Configurator will automatically assign the next available number. Type in "Fish Prep Membership" (arrow #1).

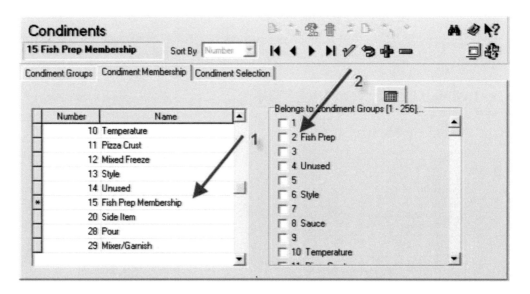

Next click on the box next to Fish Prep (arrow #2) and save using the green check mark.

## Step 2d: Defining Condiment Selection

OK. We're half way there. The next step is to define the Condiment Selection. This is where we can combine more than one set of required condiments. For example this is where we will tell the system to ask for *Fish Prep* first and then ask for a *Side Item*. Condiment Selection is how the Menu Item (the entrée) communicates with the Condiment.

Open up POS Configurator and go to Sales | Condiments and click on the third tab: Condiment Selection.

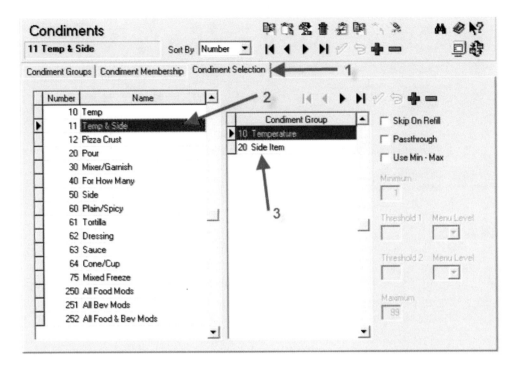

Arrow #1 shows that we're on the correct tab. Arrow #2 shows that record #11 Temp & Side references Condiment Group 10 Temperature and then Condiment Group 20 Side Item (arrow #3). The section on the left (arrow #2) is how we link a Condiment Group to the Menu Item.

Click on the top ✚ button to add a new record to the left side. POS Configurator will automatically assign the next available number. Name this, "Fish Prep & Side."

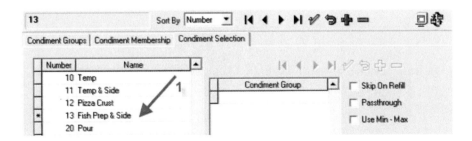

Save it with the green check mark and then go to the Condiment Group box directly to the right. Press the lower ✚ button to add a condiment group to this record.

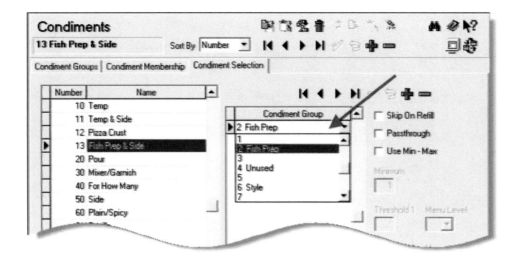

Utilizing the drop down arrow, find and select the "Fish Prep" condiment group. Save it and then click to add another Condiment Group to the list. Using the drop down box again, select the Side Item condiment group. When you are done it will look like this:

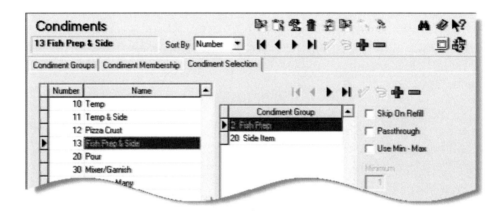

Now that we have Condiments elements of this defined it is time to connect them to our condiment menu items and to our entrée.

## Step 3: Connect Condiment Menu Items to the Condiment Membership

Now that we have completely defined our condiments in the Condiment section of the POS Configurator we need to go back and link our three condiments to the Condiment Membership.

Open POS Configurator, click on the Sales | Menu Items button. Go to the "==FISH PREP==" records we entered when we first started.

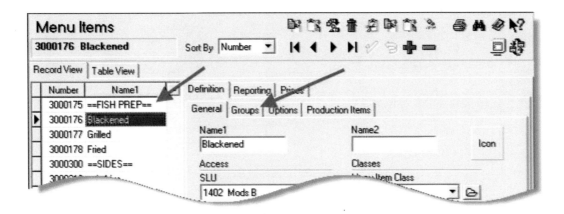

Next, click on the "Groups" tab.

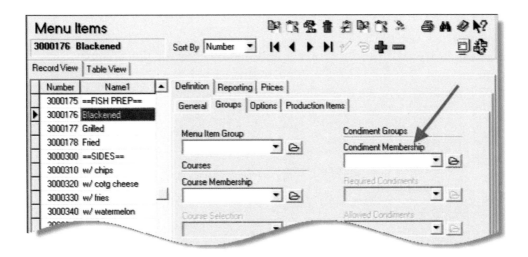

This is where we will assign "Blackened" to the Fish Prep Membership that we created earlier. Using the drop down box next to the Condiment Membership box select the "Fish Prep Membership" and don't forget to save using the green check mark.

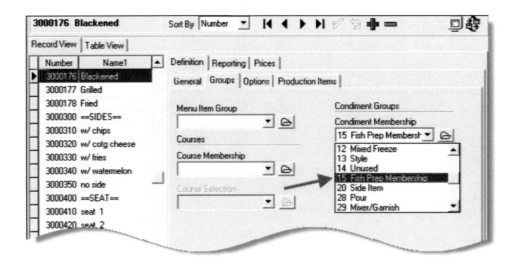

Go through the same process for each condiment that you entered earlier. In this example there are two more to set up: "Grilled" and "Fried."

## Step 4: Enter and Define the New Entrée Menu Item

In our example we still need to enter a new menu item for the Snapper. Open up POS Configurator and go to Sales | Menu Items. Find the "==SPECIALS==" header. Highlight a menu item in the Specials section and copy and paste the record.

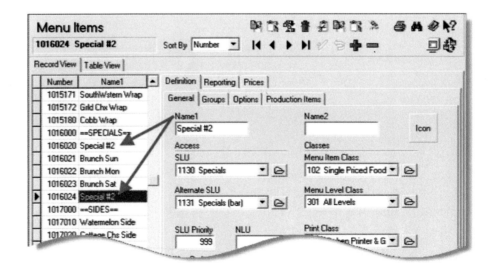

Note that we have two menu items named Special #2. Click on the new menu item in the NAVIGATION AREA and then move into the DETAIL AREA to edit it.

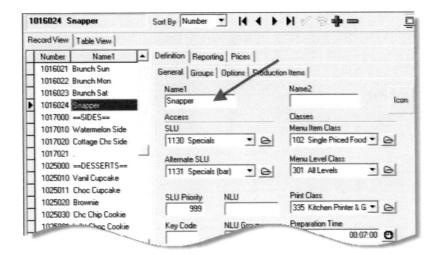

Once the name and price have been changed, take a moment to make sure that it is printing in the correct location (the kitchen), that it is showing up on the proper SLU and the reporting options are set correctly.

## Step 5: Connect the Condiment Selection to the Menu Item

After you have edited the name and the price of the menu item click on the Definition | Groups tab in the DETAIL AREA.

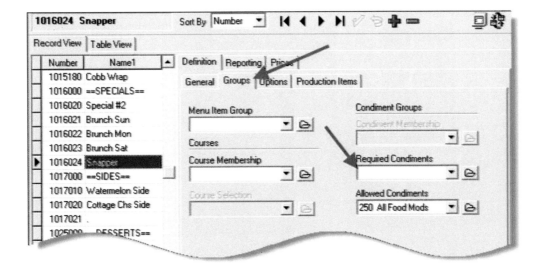

Go to the Required Condiment. Click on the drop down arrow to the right of the field (not the folder icon). From this list select "Fish Prep & Side."

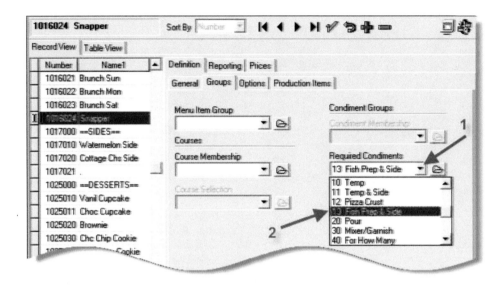

Save by clicking on the green check mark.

Congratulations! You just finished setting up a group of required Condiments / Modifiers for a Menu Item. In our example any other fish dish that this restaurant sells, setting up the prep and the sides will be simple because the system is already programmed for it.

# Allowed Condiments

This class of condiments allows the user to select options from one or more condiment groups. These are usually through the Food Modifier (or Food MODs) screens that are accessible at all times to the servers. These screens have the greatest flexibility and allow for the server to modify a Menu Item (such as an entrée or sandwich) in countless ways.

Preparation instructions are usually programmed as *allowed condiments*. This is where the "SEE SERVER" key usually resides. In order for the allowed condiments to be selected, however, a Menu Item that allows them must be ordered first. Usually these condiments are split into two main groups: Food Modifiers and Beverage Modifiers.

In the following example we are going to add a typical *allowed food condiment*. We will also revisit our Snapper entrée from earlier in order to enable *allowed condiments* to modify it.

In the following example we will add the condiment "spicy" to the Menu Item database as a condiment and then link it to the Condiment Membership Group "All Food Preps." We will then set up the Menu Item, "Snapper" to allow for All Food Preps as an allowed condiment. (Meaning that any condiment that is part of the "All Food Preps" group can be selected to modify the Snapper.)

## Step 1: Create and Define a New Allowed Condiment (Modifier)

The process of creating an allowed modifier is identical to that of creating a Required Modifier. The only difference is the Condiment Membership Group we assign it to. Rather than assign it to a specific group like "Fish Prep," we assign it to the more general group of "All Food Preps".

Open POS Configurator | Sales | Menu Items. Find the "==S MODS==" section in the database. Highlight one of the S-Mods. In our example we are going to highlight the "seafood" modifier.

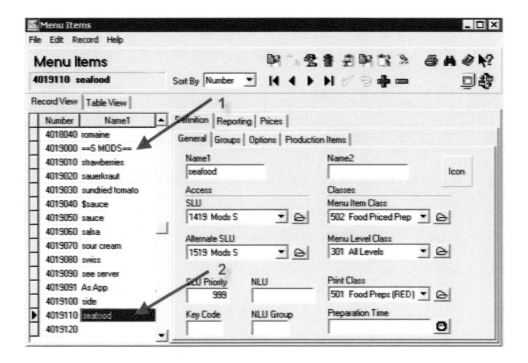

Utilize the Copy Record and Paste Record functions. POS Configurator will put the new record in the first available number.

Notice we now have 2 "seafood" modifiers. Click on the second of the two records in the NAVIGATION AREA. In the DETAIL AREA of the window change the name to "spicy". Next, check all of the options in the Definition | General tab.

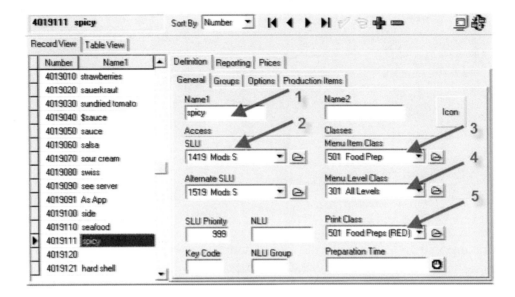

Arrow #2 shows us that it's showing up in the correct menu screen, arrow #3 shows us that it's a regular (not priced) prep, arrow #4 shows us that it's effective for all Menu Levels; and arrow #5 shows us that it prints as a red food prep. So far so good!

Next check your Prices tab to be sure that there is no price entered into the record then check your reporting tab to be sure that it reports to Food and Modifiers respectively.

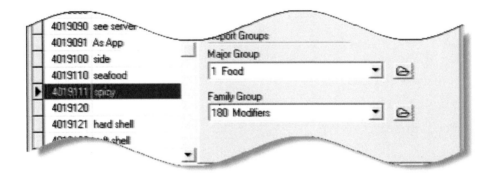

Finally go to the Definition | Groups tab. Just like our other condiments from earlier we need to assign it to a Condiment Membership Group.

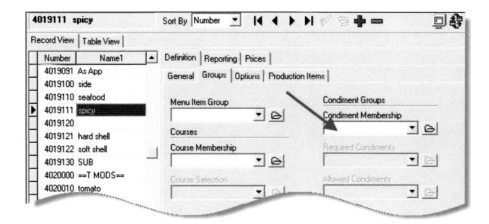

Using the drop arrow key next to the Condiment Membership field scroll until you find, "All Food Preps." Click on that and save the record.

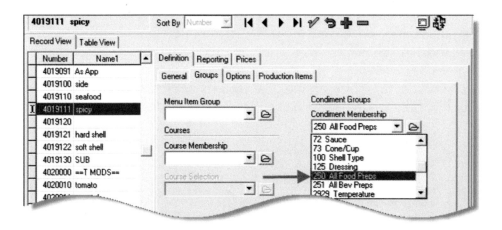

The modifier "spicy" will now show up on the SLU (Screen Look Up) of "S Mods" under the Food Modifiers screen.

## Step 2: Enabling Allowed Condiments for a Menu Item

There's only one more step to take before our new Menu Item, "Snapper" can utilize this modifier. That is to define the "All Food Preps" as an allowed condiment for our menu item.

Open up POS Configurator | Sales | Menu Items and locate the Snapper menu item. Then click on the Definition | Groups tab.

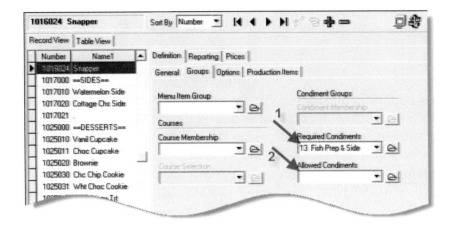

Looking at arrow #1 we can see our programming from earlier under the Required Condiments. This time we want to allow general food preps under the "Allowed Condiments."

Utilizing the drop arrow box next to the Allowed Condiments field, scroll down until you find, "All Food Mods."

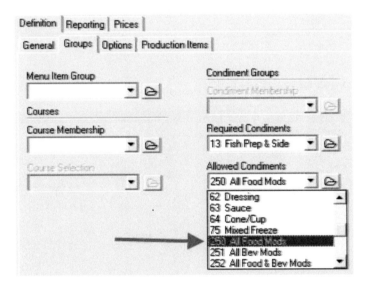

Click on 'All Food Mods' and save using the green check mark. That's all there is to it! Now when a server orders a 'Snapper Blackened' they can add the modifier 'spicy' to really take it up a notch!

# Setting the Tax Rate

In today's economy it is no surprise that tax rates around the country are on the rise. This section will show you how to go about adjusting the tax rate within the POS system. It's very straightforward and should only take a few minutes.

Start by opening up the POS Configurator. Once there go to the "Sales" tab and then click on the "Tax Rates" tab.

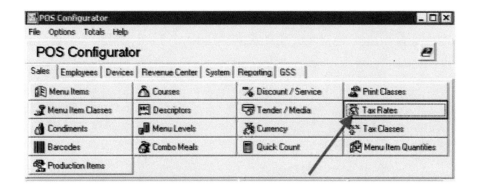

This will bring up the Tax Rates screen:

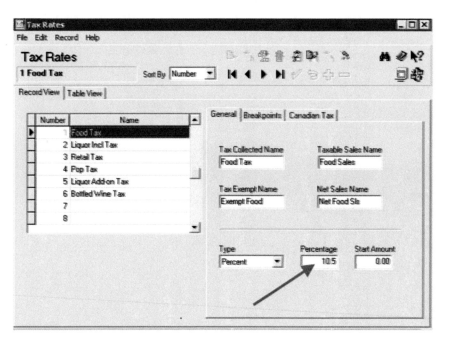

Depending on your municipality, you may have just one tax rate or you might have many. In the example above the restaurant has multiple tax rates. Simply adjust each one as needed. In the example above the tax is actually going to go down by .25%.

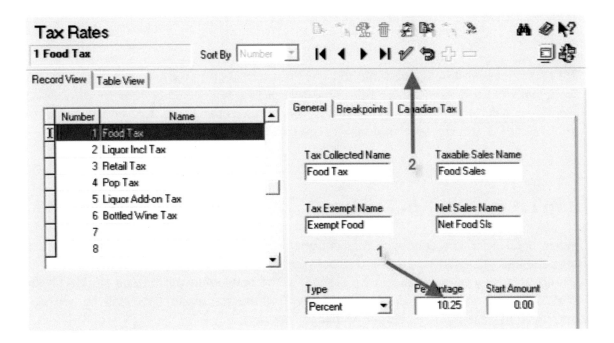

Notice that when you change the numerical value in the Percentage box, the green check mark (the "SAVE" key) and the red "UNDO" symbol become active. Once you've changed the percentage go ahead and click on the green save check mark.

Continue doing this through the appropriate taxes by highlighting them in the left navigation area and then adjusting them on the right in the detail area.

Once you've worked your way through the various tax rates on the left you're done!

# Working with Employees in the Micros System

## Adding, Changing & Terminating Employees
## Running the Payroll Report

All employees must be entered into the Micros system before they can clock in or do any work with the registers. In the following section we will go over how to enter a new employee, how to terminate an employee, how to make changes to their hourly rates, how to change their security level and how to run the payroll report.

### Step 1: Entering a New Employee

When entering a new employee it is important that you have two things. The first is an un-assigned Micros magnetic card. The second thing you will need is all of the new employee's information. This will include jobs the new employee will be working, rates, start date, and what section (revenue center) of the restaurant they will be primarily employed in (restaurant, café, lounge, bar or catering).

> **NOTE**: If your restaurant does not use Micros magnetic cards you can easily use any combination of numbers that the server will need to enter, instead of swiping in, to log onto the system to enter orders on the system.

For every employee we enter into the system we have to define the following information:

1. Jobs
2. Revenue Center
3. Assign a Magnetic Card
4. Employee Class
5. Cash Drawer
6. Start Date
7. Hourly Rates

Let's get started by opening up the POS Configurator. Once open click on the "Employees" tab. Then click on the "Employees" tab beneath it. That will bring up the "Human Resources / Employee Setup" dialogue box. It will look like this:

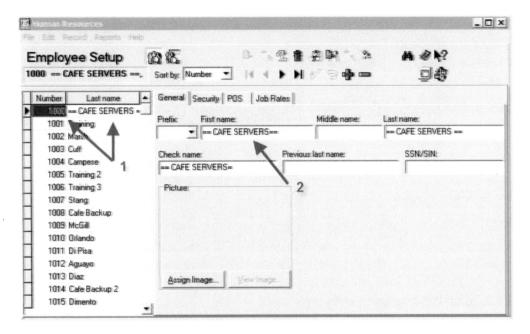

This is where we will define each employee. The list on the left (arrow #1) is the area that allows us to navigate through different employees and add new ones. We call this the **Navigation Area**. The blue box (in this case over the number 1000) indicates which employee we are looking at. We can verify that by looking in the area to the right of the list (arrow #2). This area is the **Detail Area** for the highlighted employee. In the example above employee number 1000 is highlighted on the left, the Last name is shown directly to the right of the number and in the detail area we see any particular information for this record.

Taking a closer look at the detail area we see 4 tabs at the top.

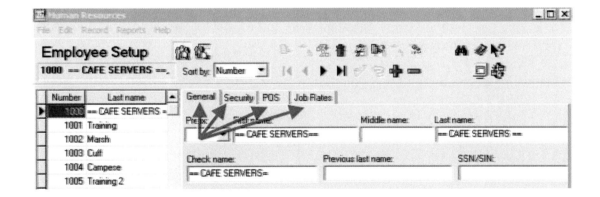

These tabs, General, Security, POS and Job Rates, allow us to define each employee so the POS system can track their hours, assign them to the correct revenue center, etc. which in turn will allow the Back Office to track labor cost and other important financial data.

We are going to add the following employee:

| | | |
|---|---|---|
| Name: | Jane Doe | |
| Jobs: | Bartender | ($5.50) |
| | Barback | ($7.50) |
| | Bar Support | ($12.00) |
| | Bar Manager | ($18.00) |

Jane Doe's primary job is going to be bartending but occasionally she'll help out managing and be doing some barback work. Because she's primarily going to be a bartender, we want to scroll down in the Navigation Area until we find the header for bartenders. This will look similar to our "==Café Servers==" header we saw when we first opened up the employee setup box.

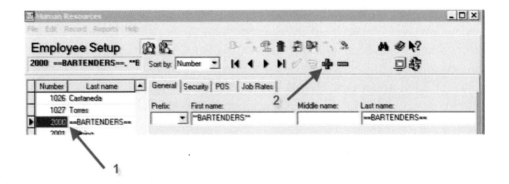

Once we find the "Bartenders" header (arrow #1), go to the last employee listed and click on the blue plus button (arrow #2). This will add a new record that we will allow us to define our new employee.

When we press that button we get the following screen:

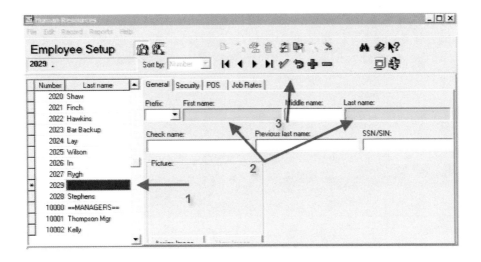

## Working with the "General" Tab

Notice in the Navigation Area we have a blank, dark blue box and in the Detail Area we have the fist and last name boxes highlighted. This indicates that the system is waiting for us to enter in the information. In the Detail Area go ahead and enter Jane Doe (Arrows #2). When you are finished, save it by clicking on the green check mark above (arrow #3). This green check mark is the Save button.

## Working with the "Security" Tab (Assigning a Micros Magnetic Card)

Next we need to enter the security information for Jane Doe. Click on the Security Tab. Notice that while the Detail Area changed, the Navigation Area did not. Your display should look like this:

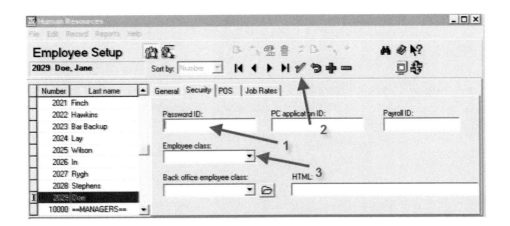

Click in the "Password ID" box (arrow #1). Now take the unassigned Micros magnetic card and slide it through the magnetic card reader that is attached to the computer. The number from the card should appear in the box. Now save using the green check mark (arrow #2).

> **NOTE**: Whether you're using Micros magnetic cards or a series of numbers for the server to clock in, Micros will not let you enter the same number for more than one person. If a duplicate number is being used the box will turn red and Micros will not allow you to save it.

Next, pull down the "Employee Class" menu by clicking on the arrow next to the box (arrow #3).

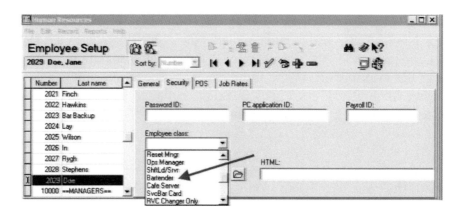

The employee class should match the primary position for the employee. This defines how the employee will interact with the Micros, what screens he or she will see and have access to and how menu items will behave. Because Jane Doe's primary duties will be bartending, go ahead and set her Employee class to Bartender. Don't forget to save with the green check mark!

If we were adding a back office manager, such as a General Manager or a Manager that needed to have access to the POS Configurator, we would fill out the "PC Application ID" field with the appropriate ID.

## Working with the "POS" Tab

Next go to the POS tab. Here is where we tell the Micros how to keep track of an employee's hours, when they started or stopped working, whether they are in training and whether they have access to a cash drawer.

### Revenue Center

The first field we want to fill out is the Revenue Center. The revenue center tells the Micros where to log the hours. This is important when running financials for the Office Manager to track labor costs and profitability of a particular area of the business.

Because Jane Doe is primarily a bartender we'll tell the Micros to consider her part of the Bar revenue center. Had her primary position been as a Café Manager, then we would have chosen the "Café" revenue center. Similarly, in a restaurant application you might have a "Lounge" revenue center or a "Banquet" revenue center.

### In Training

Training mode is useful for the new employee that is getting familiar with the Micros system and its menu layouts for the fist time. When an employee is in training mode no tickets will be printed in the kitchen or the bar, the cash drawer will not open, no credit cards will actually be charged and there will be no change in sales totals. It is important that you remember to take the employee out of training mode before their first shift!

### Cash Drawer Status

If the employee is a bartender they will need to have access to a cash drawer. If they are a server this might depend on the location. One situation where an employee other than a bartender might need access to the cash drawer would be a hostess who might need to make petty cash payouts or deal with "to go" orders. Cash drawer 2 is only used when you have two employees that share a register but not a drawer. For our example we should click the button next to cash drawer 1.

### Start and End Date

The start and end date are very important. The start date actually allows the employee to begin clocking in and out. Without a start date the employee will not be able to clock in, access any of the Micros screens, ring in items, etc.

The end date is equally important. As we will see when we run the payroll report, an employee who has been terminated or resigned will remain in the system as an active employee until an "End date" has been entered. They will not show up on the payroll but they are still technically "active." The employee will continue to show up on a "Complete Employee Listing."

For this exercise, fill in the revenue center (bar), the cash drawer and the start date. Don't forget to save using the green check mark! The Detail Area should look like this:

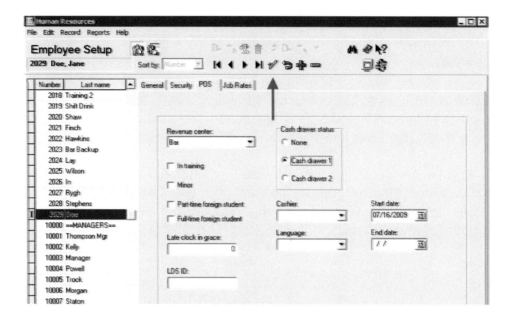

**Working with the "Job Rates" Tab**

The final step is to add the jobs that this employee will be performing. Click over to the "Job Rates" tab in the Detail Area. In order to add jobs click in the blank field under "Name." A drop down menu will appear. This will list all of the available jobs that are defined on the system. For this example, go ahead and choose "Bartender" as Jane Doe's first job (arrow #1).

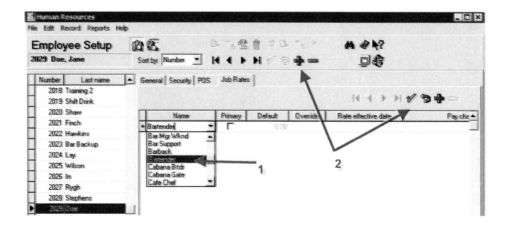

Notice that there are two different "save/undo/add new record" sets of buttons (arrow #2). The ones at the top represent the entire file for the current employee (in this case Jane

Doe). The ones to the right are specific to the list of jobs that we are creating. We will use the lower right blue "add" key for Jane Doe's additional jobs; eventually saving the entire record with the check mark at the top.

For each job we need to enter a rate. On some systems there might be a default rate. On others this might be $0.00. In any case, it's important that we utilize the "Override" field to enter the correct amount for the employee. Set the "Rate effective date" to the current date. When you've entered the rate and rate effective date, save it using the green check mark. Press the blue plus button to enter any additional jobs for the employee.

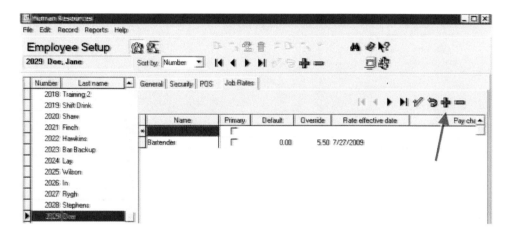

Continue this process until all of the employee's rates have been entered. Once this is complete make sure to save it!

Once you've entered all of the pay rates it should look like this:

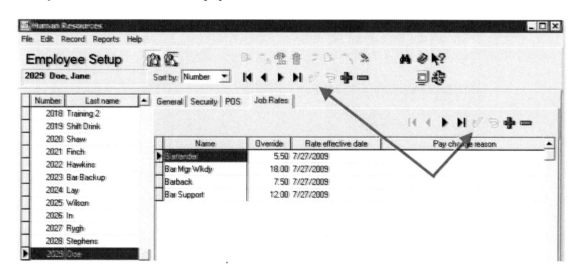

Notice that neither green check mark is visible. This indicates that the latest changes have already been saved.

Congratulations! You've just entered a new employee.

## Step 2: Terminating an Employee

When an employee is terminated or resigns, it's very important to make the proper adjustments to the POS system. The two necessary adjustments are to remove the password number from their employee record and enter an end date for the employee.

Open up POS Configurator and go to the employee tab. Open up the Employee screen and locate the particular employee. For this example we will use Jane Doe again. Once Jane Doe is visible in the Detail Screen click on the Security Tab.

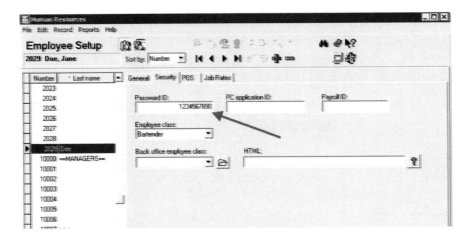

Click in the "Password ID" field and press the "DEL" key. This will clear the field. By doing this the Micros magnetic card becomes reusable. It also ensures that no one else can log in as Jane Doe and ring under her identity.

Second, click over to the POS tab and enter an end date.

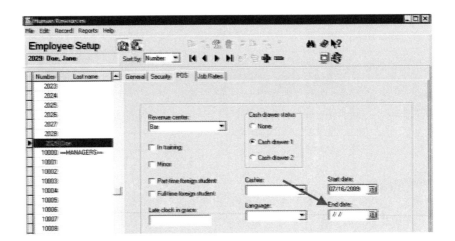

By entering an end date the employee becomes "inactive." This means that the employee will no longer show up on the "Complete Employee Listing" or the payroll. Be sure to save with the green check mark when finished.

## Step 3: Changing an Employee's Hourly Rate

Once an employee has been entered into the system making changes to their record is very easy. Utilize the Navigation Area to find the employee. Click on their file so they show up in the Detail Area. Once there you can easily go to the "Job Rates" tab and adjust their pay for a particular job or add another job. This pay rate will become effective starting the next pay period.

> *NOTE*: Once an employee has been given a job and has clocked in under it, it *can not* be removed. This is to ensure accurate record keeping and the ability, later down the line, of recalling important labor data.

## Step 4: Changing an Employee's Security Level

For businesses that promote from within, it is often necessary to give an existing employee more access to different parts of the Micros system as they take on additional responsibility. For instance – if an employee goes from a bartender position to a management position they would need access to the Manager's screen on the Micros terminals in the bar or restaurant.

In this example, simply having the job of Manager on the "Job rates" tab would be sufficient. The employee would only need to be clocked in as a manager to access those manager screens.

### Granting Back Office Access

If, however, a floor manager needed access to the back office PC it would require an additional security change in order to grant that access.

Open up POS Configurator and go to the employee tab. Open up the Employee screen and locate the particular employee. For this example we will again use Jane Doe. Once Jane Doe is visible in the Detail Screen, click on the security Tab.

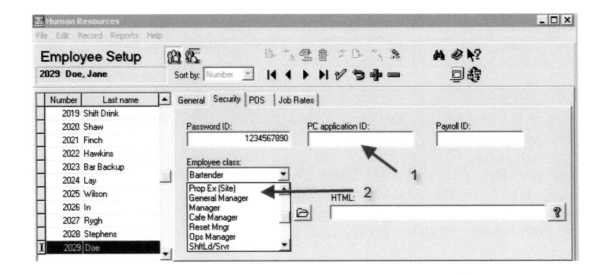

Under the field "PC Application ID" enter a numeric password. This can be the same as the employees "Password ID" from their card or it can be something unique.

The second step is to change this employee's class. In this case the employee might now have unlimited access to the system (utilizing the Prop Ex class or the GM class) or a lower level access such as a Reset Manager. This will depend on the way the system has been configured.

> **NOTE**: Employee Classes act to define parameters for a particular group of employees that behave the same. By setting up a class for each group of employee the manager has far less information to enter for each new employee.

Note that when Jane clocks in as a bartender she will still have the "Bartender Speed Screen" show up as her default. Changing the Employee class simply gives her more access to the back office PC.

## Step 5: Running the Payroll Report

On most Micros systems, the payroll report will be set up to run automatically after the close of business on the last day of the pay period. If, for some reason it fails to run or adjustments needed to be made to an employee time card after it ran, it's very easy to run manually.

After making all adjustments to employee time cards, open up "Autosequences and Reports." Depending on how your system was set up, the initial screen that comes up might be very different from the one below. Don't worry. We're going to click on the "Reports" tab and everything will be the same.

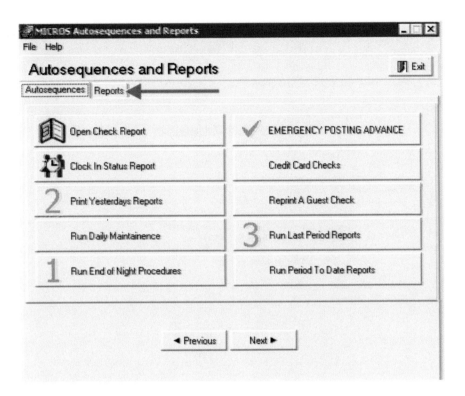

Once there click on the "Labor" button.

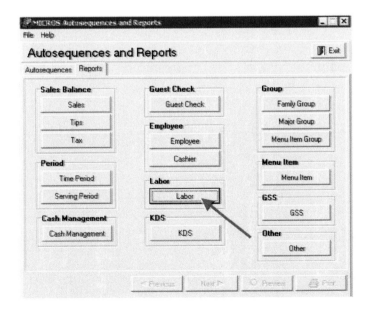

That will take you to a list of reports that are available under labor. The report that we are interested in is the "Custom – EMP Payroll Summary." Highlight that report (arrow #1) and the click on the "Next" button (arrow #2).

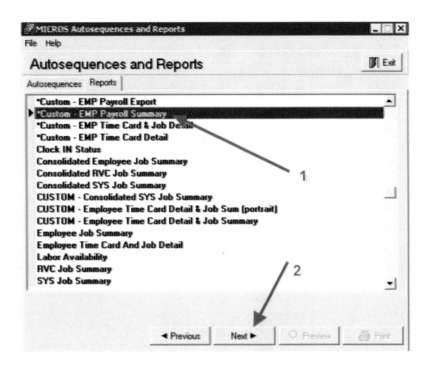

The system will now prompt for a date range. This gives us the option of pulling historical payroll records out of the system. For the sake of this exercise we are interested in the last pay period.

There are two ways to tell the system what our date range is. The first way is click on the calendar button next to the "From" field and enter the first date of the pay period (arrow #1 below).

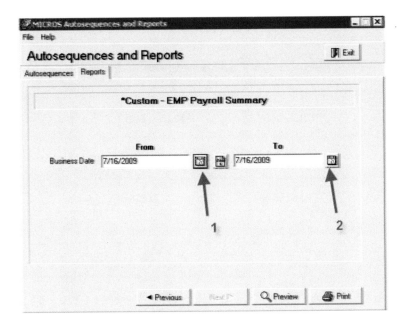

Then set the second date manually by pressing the calendar button next to the "To" field and setting it (arrow #2 above).

The second and more efficient way is to pull up some pre-set date ranges. We do this by clicking on the yellow button in between the "From" and "To" fields.

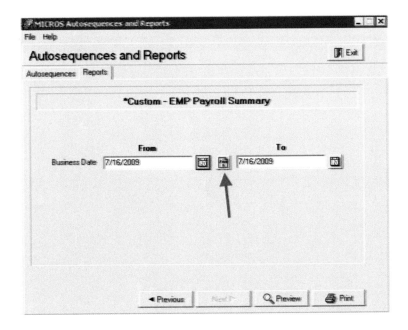

This will bring up the following screen:

Here we can select a whole bunch of different pre-determined time periods. For this exercise click on the "Last Pay Period" button and then press "OK." Now press on the "Preview" button.

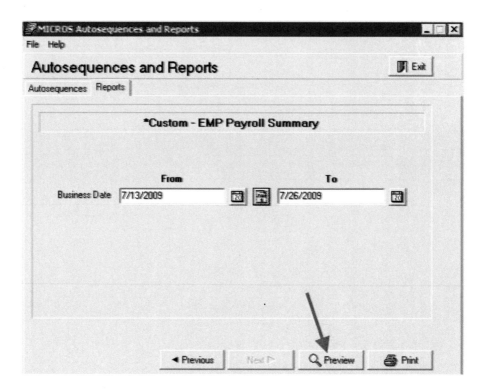

This will bring up something similar to this:

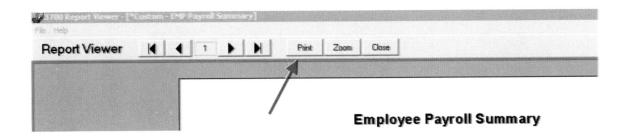

**Employee Payroll Summary**

Teaching Teaching
Period From : 05/18/2009    To : 05/31/2009                    Printed on Wednesday, May 27, 2009 - 12:46 PM

**Training, JohnDoe (40038)**

| Hours | Rate | Total |
|-------|------|-------|
| 2.03 | 5.00 | 10.15 |
| 2.04 | 5.50 | 11.22 |
| 3.06 | 8.00 | 24.48 |
| 2.04 | 9.00 | 18.36 |
| 2.01 | 10.00 | 20.10 |

| Job Totals | Regular Hours | Overtime Hours | Regular Pay | Overtime Pay | Total Pay |
|------------|---------------|----------------|-------------|--------------|-----------|
| 1001 - Barback | 2.04 | | 5.61 | 0.00 | 5.61 |
| 1002 - Expediter | 1.02 | | 8.16 | 0.00 | 8.16 |
| 1005 - Bar Support | 2.04 | | 8.16 | 0.00 | 8.16 |
| 1008 - Cabana Gate | 2.01 | | 10.10 | 0.00 | 10.10 |
| 3000 - Cafe Server | 2.03 | | 5.05 | 0.00 | 5.05 |
| 3004 - Cafe Support | 2.04 | | 9.36 | 0.00 | 9.36 |
| | 11.18 | 0.00 | 46.44 | 0.00 | 46.44 |

Next, after verifying the dates are correct, press the "Print" button at the top of the report.

Now simply close out of the report and exit out of the report viewer.

# Working with Jobs

This section will deal with creating new Jobs within the Micros POS. Jobs are what the employees must clock in under. It is within the Jobs framework that certain positions are grouped together for labor reporting. The Jobs Dialogue box is where all Jobs are defined for all Employees across the system. Before a job can be accessed in the Employees Dialogue box, it must be defined here.

Jobs can be set up to have a default hourly wage, be linked to other Jobs in order to more precisely track a department's labor cost (through Job Category) and be linked to a pre-defined Time Clock Schedule. At the very least each Job has to have labor category that will be used by the system for labor reports.

In the following example we will create a new Job called, "Beach Bartender." The default hourly rate will be $4.25/ hr, the job will require the employee to declare their tips at the end of the shift and they will belong to the Bar revenue center.

Open up POS Configurator. Go to Employees | Jobs.

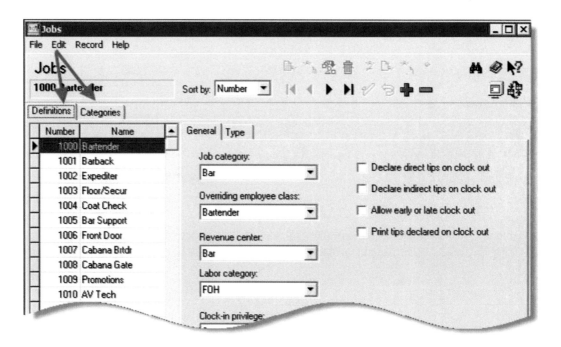

Notice that there are two tabs in the NAVIGATION AREA – Definitions and Categories. 'Definitions' contains a list of all of the defined Jobs in the system. This is where we will be adding our new Job of Beach Bartender.

Categories allows more concise grouping of particular jobs.

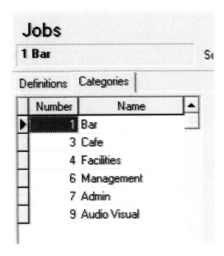

If we wanted to, as per our example, we could put Beach Banquet down as a category and more closely track what the labor costs for the new beach expansion would be. Other applications of Categories might be to place all of the prep cook positions in one category under the Back of House overall labor category.

Click back over to the Definitions tab and highlight the job that the new position will most closely resemble. In this case 'Bartender.'

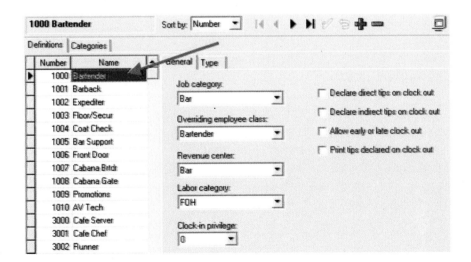

Go ahead and copy and paste the record so we have an identical record for Bartender.

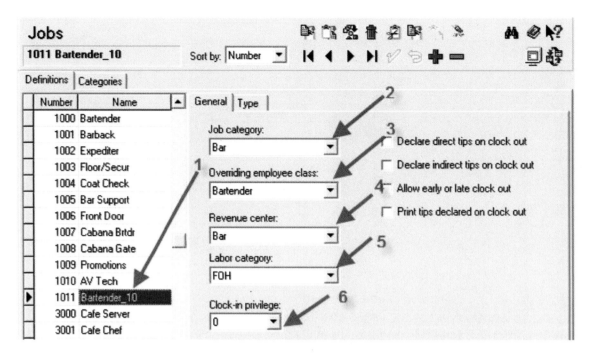

First we'll want to change the name in the Definition field to 'Beach Bartender.'

## Job Category

Next (arrow #2) we see that we can choose a Job Category for the beach bartender. If we were categorizing the beach labor separately, this is where we would choose it from the drop down list.

## Overriding Employee Class

Arrow #3 is where we attach an 'Overriding Employee Class.' Set that to the new Employee Class we designated in the last exercise (Working with Employee Classes) to 'Banquet Bartender.' The employee class that we put in this box will override an employee's normal class when working this job. All this means is that the employee, when clocked in as 'Beach Bartender' will have all of the privileges associated with the 'Banquet Bartender' class.

## The Revenue Center

The Revenue Center is used to track costs and revenue. Depending on your set up this could be Bar, Lounge, Café, Restaurant, Catering, etc. In our example we would set this to Beach, Café or Restaurant. This will depend on how your enterprise is set up.

## Labor Category

The Labor Category is the overriding category. Unlike the Job category that allows us to set smaller labor designations, this one deals with the bigger labor picture for the enterprise. Choices are FOH (Front of House), BOH (Back of House), Admin, and Managers. For our example we will use FOH.

## Clock-in Privilege

Clock in privilege references the privileges from the Employee Class dialogue. If we set it to 0 there are no restrictions on clocking in and out. If you set it to 1 or 2 a manager would have to be present when an employee is clocking in. Many restaurants use this option when setting up a food prep position so that a manager has to be present when an employee clocks in. This is useful if there is concern that one employee is clocking another in before they actually are there and ready to begin their shift.

## Options

Check the appropriate options on the right to have the employee declare tips on clock out. If the new employee is a barback or other indirectly tipped employee choose the 'Declare indirect tips' on the right.

This is what the Beach Bartender looks like when we're done:

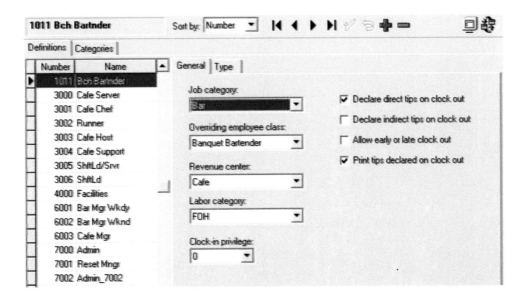

Click over to the "Type" tab:

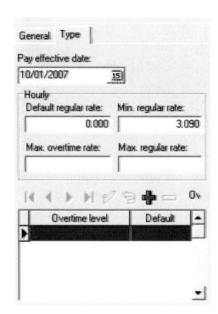

This tab is where you can set default hourly wage values for this job. You can also set up Overtime levels and defaults.

Once you're done with the different setting in the Jobs dialogue box save it with the green check mark. Now that Job is available when you add a new employee and go to define the jobs they will be working.

# Employee Classes

Employee Classes allow the operator to control every aspect of the manner in which an employee interacts with the system. Employee classes allow the restaurant operator the ability to change whole groups of employees at the same time with ease. An example of an Employee Class might be Manager, General Manager, Bartender, etc. By setting up an Employee Class for each major position in the restaurant it greatly simplifies the process of adding new employees or changing the privileges of a whole group of employees at one time.

In this section we will add a new Employee Class and go through the options that you, as an Operator, are most likely to have to change.

> *NOTE*: Making changes to the Employee Class is <u>NOT</u> recommended. This section is included in the book for the more advanced user who feels comfortable with programming the Micros POS. A new Employee Class should only be created if the existing classes are not adequate. For example – if the business has expanded and there is a need for a class of worker with slightly different privileges.

## Before Getting Started

Entering a new Employee Class can be complicated when creating it from scratch because there are hundreds of options to set. Before beginning, therefore, take the time to think about the new position. As far as the position's interaction with the POS System, what position currently being used is closest to it? It will save immeasurable time if there is a position you can use as a base to work from. Then take the time to think about how this new position needs to be different. Write these factors out on a sheet of paper before getting started. Once in the system the options can be overwhelming.

For this exercise we are going to create an Employee Class for the new position of Banquet Bartender. Our fictitious restaurant has expanded and started doing banquets on the beach. Both the servers and the bartenders out on the beach have to share a terminal. Therefore the Bartenders will behave very much like the ones inside the restaurant, but because they are sharing a register it will be necessary to have the system sign them out of their screen every time they complete a transaction. As a new enterprise, the Owner doesn't expect the bar to be full from the start and therefore wants to be able to track the number of covers done on the beach. Therefore they want the Banquet Bartender to be forced to enter the number of customers they serve at both the bar and the few bar tables.

Before opening up Touchscreen Designer we know the following:

- The new Employee Class will behave very similar to the 'Bartender' class

- The following changes will need to be made:

    o Banquet Bartender class will need to be automatically signed out after each transaction

    o Banquet Bartender must be forced to enter number of covers before beginning a check

Just two changes! This should be a breeze! Let's get started!

# Programming a New Employee Class

Open up POS Configurator. Go to Employees | Employee Classes.

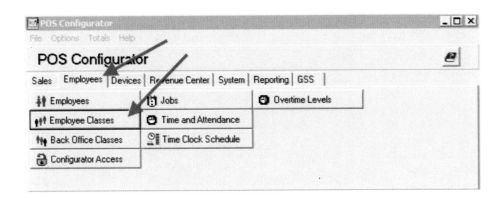

That will bring up the Employee Classes Dialogue Box:

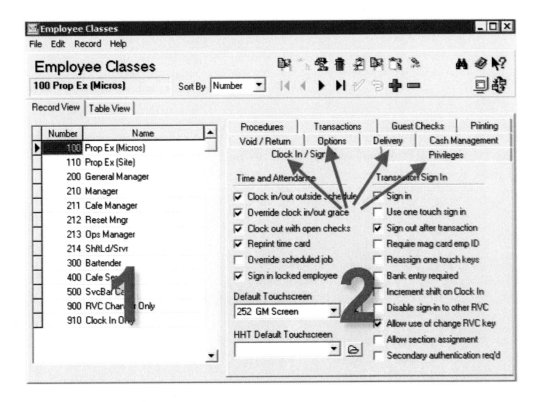

This dialogue box is similar to the others in POS Configurator. On the left (number 1) is the NAVIGATION AREA. On the right (number 2) is the DETAIL AREA. Notice how many different tabs and options there are in the detail area. Yikes! This is why it's so important to take time to think about the changes you want to make before hand.

For our example, we're going to be emulating the 'Bartender' class. Locate the Bartender class in the NAVIGATION AREA and highlight it. This will bring up the detail information on the right.

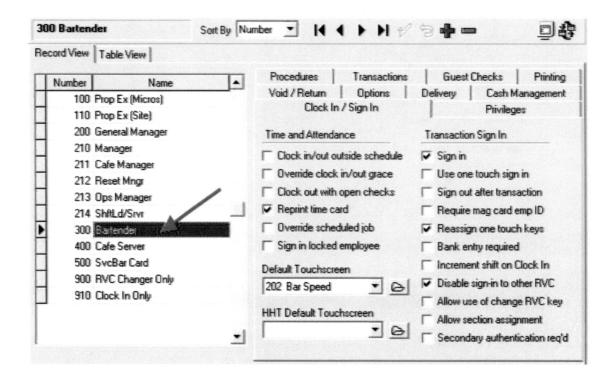

Thankfully, we don't have to manually copy all of the information into a blank record. Making sure that only one of the two fields is highlighted on the left, go up to the Edit menu and click on 'Copy Record.' Then click on 'Paste Record.'

We now have two identical records. Let's go ahead and rename the bottom one 'Banquet Bartender.' Now the only thing to do is to go and find the two elements that we want to change from the other bartenders that will make this Employee Class unique.

> ***TIP***: Take some time to look at the different tabs and all of the choices that are there. This is where all of the options are set for all employees. There are so many options because the Employee Class has to have every available option no matter what the type of employee. The Context Sensitive Help **♦?** is very helpful in this situation. Click on it once and then click on the option to get an explanation.

For the sake of our example we're interested in just two of the hundred or so choices.

With the 'Banquet Bartender' highlighted in the NAVIGATION AREA, go to the 'Clock In / Sign In' tab in the DETAIL AREA.

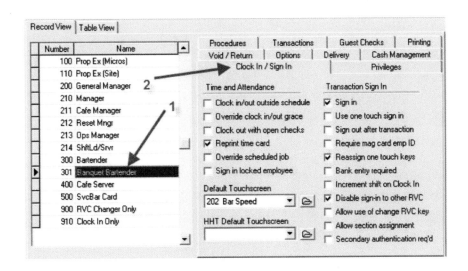

In order to have the system sign the bartender out after the transaction we need to find the correct radio box. (A radio box is an on/off box that either is blank or has a check mark in it). Once you have found, "Sign out after transaction" put a check mark next to it and save with the green check mark at the top.

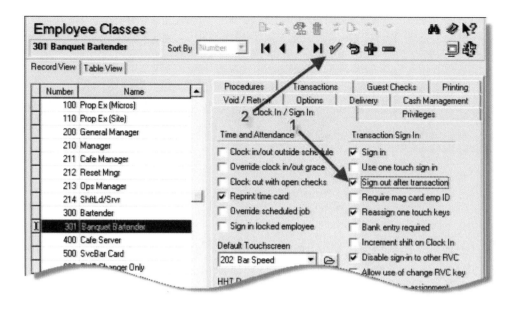

The second element that we need to change is to have the system prompt the Banquet Bartender for the number of covers. If we think it through slowly we realize that we are asking the system to ask for a required entry. Taking it a step further, the system is going to ask for a required entry on each transaction.

Click on the Transactions | Required Entries tab in the DETAIL AREA.

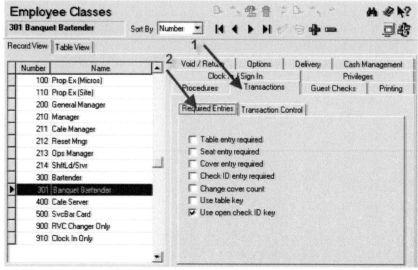

Once there look down the list until you find, 'Cover entry required.' Check the box. This will cause the system to prompt for the number of covers at the table or bar before the Banquet Bartender can begin the order process.

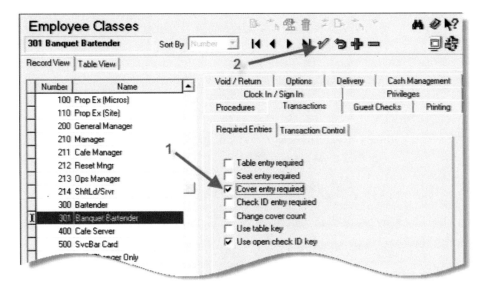

The Employee Class has a tremendous amount of power. This is where every possible behavior between an Employee and the system is defined. There are few times when a normal operator would need to make changes to this element of the POS system but it helps to be familiar in case the occasion does arise.

## Clock In / Sign In

As mentioned in the tutorial above, this is where you'll set the default Touchscreen for an employee class.

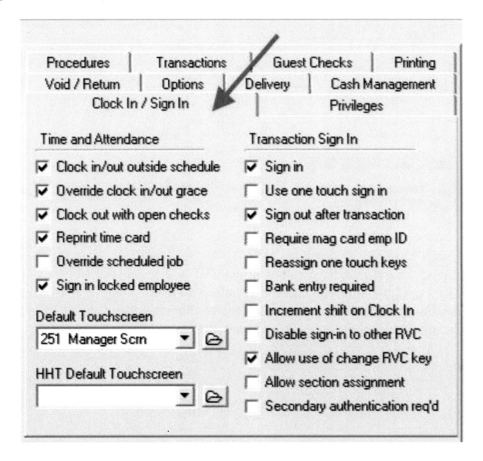

This is also the place where you set the default Touchscreen if using Hand Held Devices. The options you set here directly affect how and if an Employee can gain access to the system.

## Privileges

Privileges are based on a 4 point system. 3 is the highest and usually reserved for the Property Expert or General Manager. 2 is High and usually used for Management and Head Waiters. 1 is Low and usually used for Kitchen Staff and Bus Persons. And 0 is No Restrictions. Access to this key is not restricted.

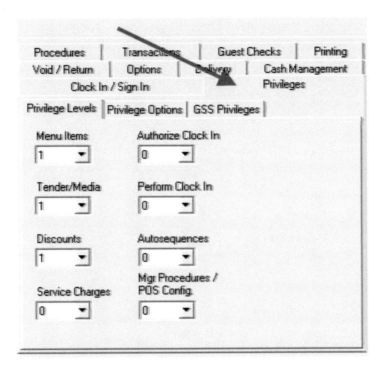

Depending on the environment of your establishment, you might use all 4 levels of privileges or less. Many bars and nightclubs, for instance, use only three because they do not have as complicated as a set up as a restaurant with banquets, a dining room, a bar, etc.

## Procedures

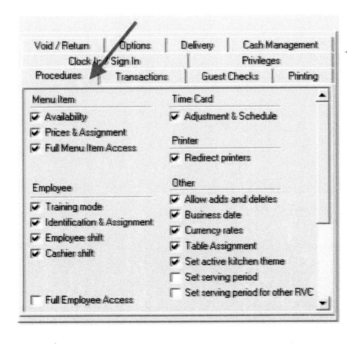

Under procedures you can set whether an employee class can set menu item availability, adjust time cards, put an employee in and take them out of training mode, and whether or not they can redirect printers.

## Transactions

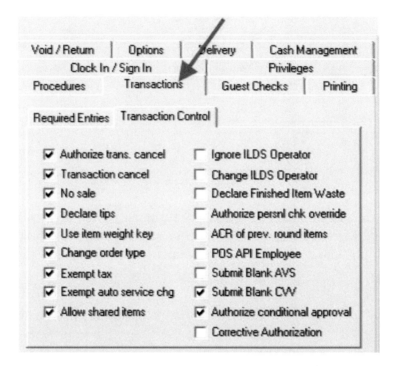

The Transactions tab allows the Operator to define required actions such as table number entry, number of covers, seat numbers, etc. It also allows the Operator to control whether the employee can cancel transactions, do a 'No Sale,' declare tips on clock out, and many other choices.

## Guest Checks

Guest Checks has multiple tabs. This is where check splitting, transferring, re-opening checks and editing checks is all handled.

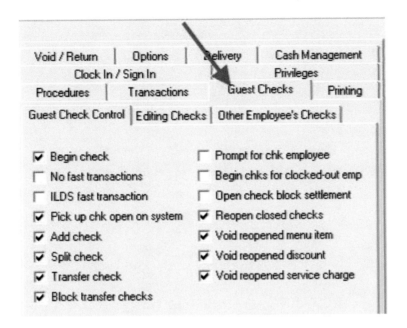

For instance, you might want to allow the servers to Pickup Checks and Begin Checks, but not to 'Pick Up Others Checks.' That functionality might be reserved for the Manager.

## Printing

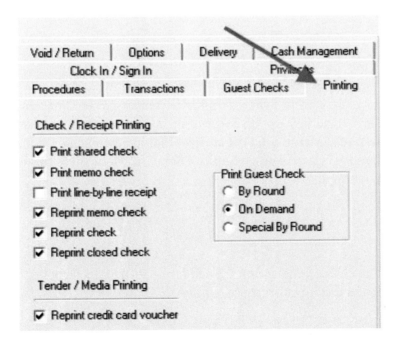

This dialogue box controls all of the printing options for an Employee Class. In the image above, the active Employee Class can print guest checks on demand. The system will not print one every round.

## Void / Return

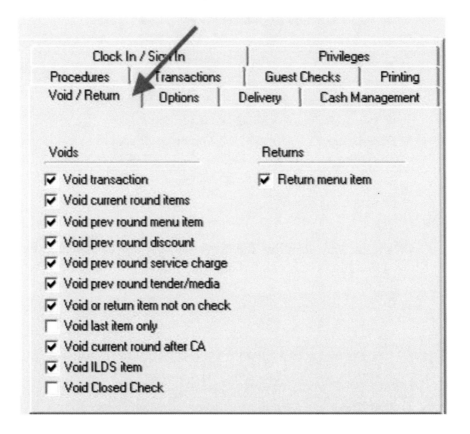

The Void / Return tab is useful when defining bartenders, wait staff and host staff that are doing to-go orders. One key option to keep an eye on is the 'Void current round after CA.' This allows the server to void off an item that had been entered in the current round but not sent. If your system is not set up to "Send" a check after an authorization you'll want to set this option to off.

## Options

There are quite a few parameters on the Options tab that an Operator might find useful when creating or modifying an existing Employee Class.

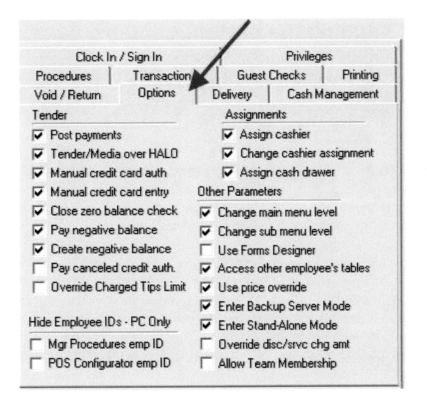

The most useful options to set in this dialogue box are usually the ability to 'Assign cash drawer' and 'Manual credit card auth.' Again, depending on the individual restaurant these parameters might be set differently from server to bartender to manager.

> **TIP**: Take some time to look at the different tabs and all of the choices that are there. This is where all of the options are set for all employees. There are so many options because the Employee Class has to have every available option no matter what the type of employee. The Context Sensitive Help ▶? is very helpful in this situation. Click on it once and then click on the option to get an explanation.

# Changing the Bartender Speed Screen

## Adjusting Hard Coded Buttons

The BARTENDER SPEED SCREEN is designed to put the most popular items in the most convenient place, grouped together with similar items, in order to; (1) Speed up the bartender; (2) Increase accuracy while reducing mistakes; and (3) Increase customer service by freeing up more time for interaction with the customer.

The purpose of this exercise is to learn how to make changes to static screens within Micros (screens that never change their button structure) that use *Hard Coded* buttons to ring in menu items. *Hard Coded* buttons are those that never change position on a menu screen. The screen that the bartenders use the most – the Bar Speed Screen – is the best example of this. In this particular example we will be changing the Bar Speed Screen to reflect product changes as well as bartender and management preferences that have changed.

This example deals with a changing product list that requires the re-arrangement of the static buttons to be more functional, user friendly and efficient. In this particular case the business has, over time, added more "IMPORT" products at the same time as eliminating some "DOMESTIC" products. This has left us with an imbalanced, messy and inefficient speed screen.

While this unorganized screen is not an issue for more veteran employees, it proves a great challenge to new employees who are struggling to learn a new system and menu already. Therefore, the purpose of this change is to make the screen more universal so both new and veteran employees move more quickly and efficiently to the appropriate area to ring in the correct items. The goal of having like items grouped together is twofold: (1) To make the bartender more efficient when ringing in orders; (2) Minimize mistakes created by a confusing interface that has like items spread randomly across the screen.

Before we get started, let's take a look at a before and after snapshot of the speed screen. The image below is the "Before" image:

| Ready For Your Next Entry | | Red Bull & RB SF | Perrier | Orange Blast | Pear Pleasure | Sexx Pitcher | |
|---|---|---|---|---|---|---|---|
| | | Fiji Water | Juice | Marg Freeze | Rasp Freeze | | |
| Apr29'09 08:58PM | Wed | Smirnoff Ice | Soda / Coffee | Martini/ Mnhttn | LIT | Bac / Grape Bomb | Sign Out |
| | | Blue Moon | Hacker Pschorr | Bloody | Double Spcl | Berg Pours | Cancel |
| | | MGD 64 | Newcast | O'Douls | Magic #9 | Wine | Void |
| | | Mich Ultra | Berry Weiss | Dos Equis | Sam Season | Cordials & Shots | Payment Screen |
| | | Bud | Leine Lmnade | Summer Shandy | Harp | Beer Pitchers | Function Screen |
| | | Bud Light | Hein | Shock Top | Guinness | Pick Up Tab | Food Screens |
| | | Bud Lt. Lime | Corona | Bud Light Drft | Half Acre | Start Tab | Bar Speed Screen |
| | | MGD | Amstel Light | Miller Lite Drft | Stella Artois | CC Sale | |
| | | Miller Lite | Red Bull Up $ | Bartndr Comp | CC Close | Send | |
| | | Jager | SF Red Bull Up $ | Shift Drink | NO SALE | Print | |
| | | Schnapps | $ 1 Up Charge | Orange Comp | | ENTER (yes) | |
| | | Premium Schnapps | Closed Chks | Emp Dis | CASH | CLEAR (no) | |

Let's take a close look at this. Starting in the upper left corner there are 5 light blue buttons with black lettering. These are all similar in that they are non-alcohol drinks (Red Bull, Perrier, Fiji, Juice, and Soda). Moving down the left column we see two dark blue buttons and then a line of yellow buttons. The dark blue buttons jog over to the second column and then continue down. The dark blue buttons represent an IMPORT price. Whereas the yellow buttons represent a DOMESTIC price. Wouldn't it be better if we could somehow put all of those Blue buttons in the same general space?

Now let's look to the right four columns over. Do you see the magenta buttons with black lettering? (Magic #9, Dos Equis, etc)? These are import priced draft beers. The three green buttons directly to the left of these are domestic draft beers. Couldn't these be arranged better?

Now let's take a look at the "After" image:

| Ready For Your Next Entry | | Fiji Water | Red Bull & RB SF | Marg Freeze | Cosmo Pitcher | | |
|---|---|---|---|---|---|---|---|
| | | Perrier | Soda / Coffee | Orange Blast | Jagrbmb Spcl | | |
| | | Juice | Smirnoff Ice | Pear Pleasure | | | Sign Out |
| Bar | Tue | O'Douls | Blue Moon | Rasp Rush | Martini/ Mnhttn | Bac / Grape Bomb | Cancel |
| | | Mich Ultra | Newcast | Shock Top | Double Spcl | Bloody Ptch Spcl | Void |
| | | Bud | Berry Weiss | Bud Light Drft | Double Bloody | Cordials & Shots | Berg Pours |
| | | Bud Light | Hein | Miller Lite Drft | LIT | Beer Pitchers | Wine |
| | | Bud Lt. Lime | Corona | Magic #9 | Sam Season | Start Tab | Payment Screen |
| | | MGD | Amstel Light | Harp | Guinness | Pick Up Tab | Function Screen |
| | | MGD 64 | Hacker Pschorr | Dos Equis | Half Acre | CC Sale | Food Screens |
| | | Miller Lite | Leine Lmnade | Summer Shandy | Stella Artois | CC Close | Bar Speed Screen |
| | | Jager | Red Bull Up $ | Bartndr Comp | NO SALE | | |
| | | Schnapps | SF Red Bull Up $ | Orange Comp | | | Send |
| | | Premium Schnapps | $ 1 Up Charge | Emp Dis | CASH | | Print |

Notice how the buttons have been moved around to group similar items. This will result in better performance – especially from new employees who are learning the system for the first time. It provides consistency and simplicity so the employees can focus on what's really important – customer service.

So how did we get there?

In order to re-design a static screen it is necessary to do four things:

1. Define the new menu items in the database for each product that will be represented on the screen.
2. Make all old items that are no longer being sold "inactive" within the database
3. Remove all unused items from the hard keys on the speed screen
4. Redefine the hard keys within the database to represent the new products

## Step 1: Define the New Menu Items

For a detailed walkthrough of how to add and define new menu items, please see the manual titled, "How to Define a New Menu Item."

> ***TIP***: While entering all new items, be sure to jot down on a piece of scratch paper the menu item numbers for the new menu items. This will be helpful in step four.

## Step 2: Make All Old Items Inactive

For a detailed walkthrough of how to make old items inactive, please see the manual titled, "Making Menu Items Active / Inactive"

# Introduction to Touchscreen Designer

In this step we will be working with the devices tab in the POS Configurator. Once you've opened the POS Configurator click on the "Devices" tab. Then click on the "Touchscreen Designer" tab. It will look similar to this:

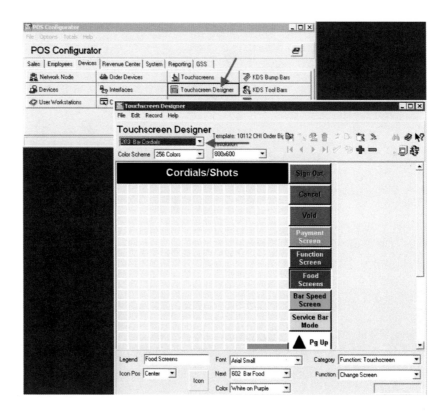

In the image above the second red arrow points to a navigation field. This drop down box allows us to navigate through all of the different screens that have been programmed in the POS system. In this particular case the screen we are looking at is the "Bar Cordials" screen.

Notice the blank grid that makes up most of the screen that looks like graph paper. This is the area that *Soft Coded* buttons will show up. When we program a menu item we usually define an SLU for it (Screen Look Up). That SLU tells it which screen to appear on. So in the example above if we were to program a cordial such as "Bailey's" and tell it to show up on the SLU for cordials, it would appear in the blank, graph paper like area above.

On the right side of the screen above are the *Hard Coded* buttons. These are the static buttons that never change position. Many times these buttons take us to a different screen such as a "Payment Screen" or a different food screen. Now let's go find the "Bar Speed Screen."

Go up to the navigation area we talked about before. Click on the arrow so the drop down appears. Then locate the "Bar Speed Screen" and click on it.

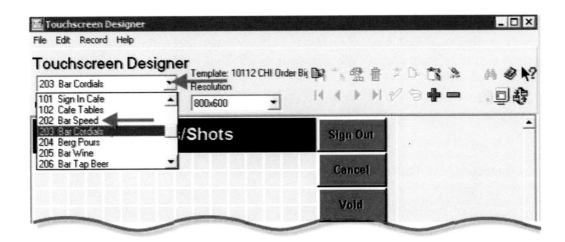

Once you have done that you will have something similar to the image below:

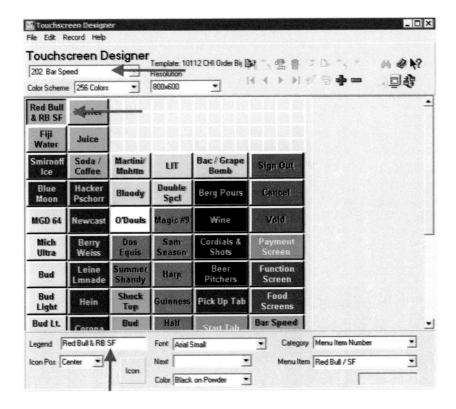

Taking a quick overview look at this screen we realize that there is very little of the open, "graph paper" type of space. Instead, most of the screen is taken up with *Hard Coded* buttons that never change position. This is the case for bartenders because they don't have to enter modifiers for drinks and need to be very fast – accessing products directly without going through multiple menu screens.

Looking at the top red arrow, we can see that we are currently looking at the "Bar Speed" screen. Looking at the red arrow on the bottom we can see that we're currently highlighting the "Red Bull & RB SF" button. Now look closely at the middle red arrow. It's pointing to the "Red Bull & RB SF" key. Notice how that square button looks slightly different from the others around the border? That's because it's highlighted.

Directing our attention back down to the bottom of the screen we see the definition area of the Touchscreen Designer. This is where we are able to define the *Hard Coded* buttons.

| | |
|---|---|
| Legend: | This is the text we want to appear on the button. |
| Icon Pos: | This is the icon position. It allows us to center the text on the button or place it to the left or right position. Similar to formatting a document. |
| Font: | The way the text looks. |
| Next: | Not used for this example. This would be used if we were working on coding a button that would take us to a different screen like a different menu screen. |
| Color: | How you want the text to appear. |
| Category: | For this example we will leave this set to "Menu Item Number." |
| Menu Item: | This is where we define what menu item the system calls when we press the hard coded button we have highlighted. |

> *TIP*: If you're curious to see what the different types of buttons there are, click on the drop down arrow area in the category field. Here you can get an idea of all the different types of categories Micros utilizes. In most cases the only category you'll need to know is the Menu Item category.

## Step 3: Removing Unused Items from the Touchscreen

In this exercise we will be switching the position of two buttons. We are going to put the "Soda / Coffee" button where the "Smirnoff Ice" button is and vice versa.

In order to do this we will have to first remove the identities of the two buttons.

Highlight the "Smirnoff Ice" button.

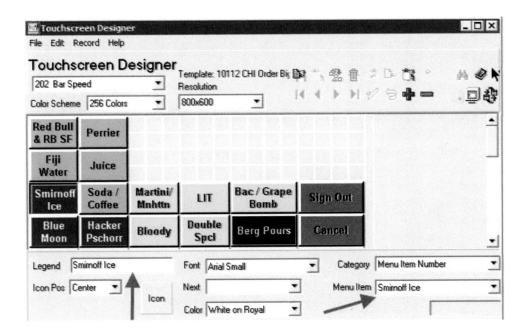

We know that "Smirnoff Ice" is the active button because its name is in the Legend field in the definition area. It's referencing the "Smirnoff Ice" menu item as the arrow to the right shows us. Click in each field and press the DELETE key. Now the screen will show the following.

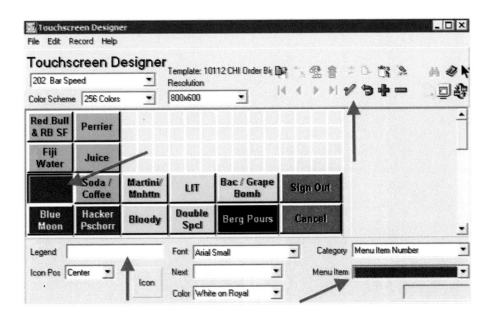

Notice that the button is blank, the menu item is blank and the Legend is blank. Click on the green check mark to save. Congratulations! You've just removed an unused menu item from the speed screen.

Continue doing that for any other menu items you want to remove. In the example below, the "Soda / Coffee" button has been removed as well.

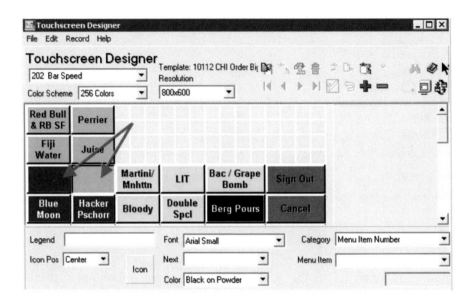

## Step 4: Redefining the Hard Keys

Now that we've eliminated the keys we no longer need, it's time to re-define them to something that we do need. In the following example we will add a different beer button for Kalik beer in a bottle and a button for Chocolate Milk.

First let's add the Chocolate Milk button. We want to put it under the "Fiji Water" button because it has similar characteristics: it's a non-alcoholic drink. We also want to try and streamline the Beer buttons so moving the beer over to the right one position will allow us to reach both goals.

Click on the button below the "Fiji Water" button. Highlight the Legend field in the definition section of Touchscreen Designer and type in, "Choc Milk."

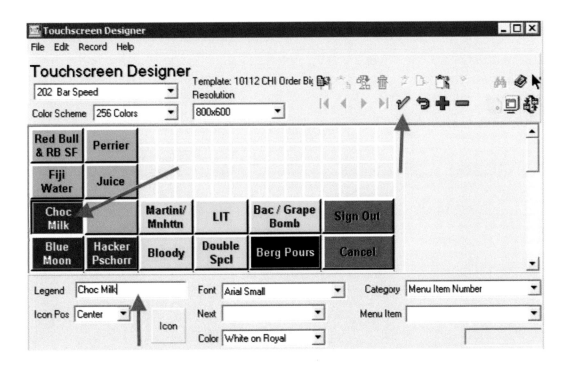

Don't forget to save your changes as you go. Now we want to make the key look like the other non-alcoholic buttons. To do this we will need to change the color.

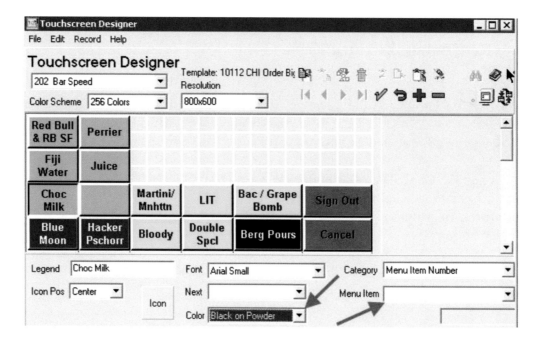

Notice that the button now has the same color and says "Choc Milk." Are we done yet? No. Notice that this button doesn't reference a menu item yet. So if you were to press it at a terminal it wouldn't work. Click in the box next to "Menu Item" in the definition section of the Touchscreen Designer. It brings up the entire menu item database in a list.

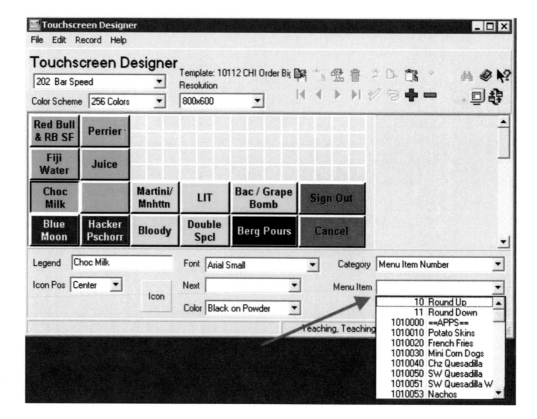

Scroll through the list until you find the item that you want this button to reference. In this case it would be "Chocolate Milk."

> **TIP**: Did you remember to write down the menu item numbers in Step 1 as you entered them? If so you can jump right to the correct item number in the drop down list without taking the time to scroll through the thousands of items there!

Save it by clicking on the green check mark. Congratulations! You've just re-defined a *Hard Coded* key! Continue doing this for all the keys necessary. In our example we will now follow the same process to re-define the key to the right of "Chocolate Milk" to read "Kalik," to reference the "Kalik" menu item, and to look like the other beer buttons below it.

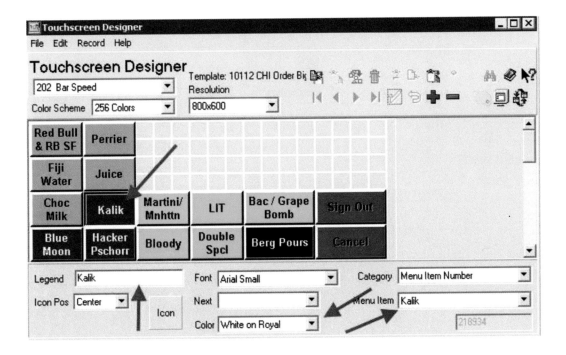

That's all there is to it! Now, whenever we need to change a beer out or any other menu item key, it can be done quickly and efficiently with minimal time.

# Autosequences & Reports

There are two places that reports can be run. They can be run from both the terminals in the restaurant as well as the back office server. This chapter will give an overview of running reports from the back office server.

The Autosequences & Reports application is where the majority of the reporting is done. This program is the interface that allows you to pull historical information from the database. Besides the reports that run automatically, any information that you need to pull out of the database system is accessible through this application.

Through Autosequences and Reports all labor, sales, employee, menu item, tip and tax reports are accessible.

Open up Autosequences & Reports. There should be an icon on the desktop that looks like this:

After entering your password, you will get the home screen of the program. Do not worry if yours does not look like this. This screen is almost always customized for each individual install.

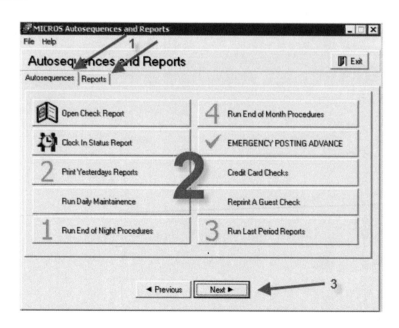

At the top of the dialogue box are two tabs (arrow #1). The first tab is the 'Autosequences' tab. The second is the 'Reports' tab. When the program is first opened it will show the 'Autosequences' tab.

> ***NOTE***: Autosequences are groups of individual reports that have been set to run together. The parameters have all been pre-defined (such as date and menu items). For example: an Autosequence might be set up to print the sales numbers of every item on the 1$^{st}$ day of the month for the previous month. This could be followed by a payroll report for the same time period.
>
> In contrast, the Report tab allows the user to define precise parameters for an individual report to look at specific information. For example: a manager wants to find out how a particular menu item sold over the course of one week. They would then run a sales report and define the parameters so that only that menu item appeared and only the sales for the week in question.

## The Autosequences Tab

The area labeled '2' in the above image is a list of quick selections that have been custom programmed for the restaurant. These will usually be set up to run the most common reports. Each of these buttons runs an "Autosequence" that has been pre-programmed in the database.

Below that are two buttons to navigate to additional screens where more custom Autosequences are listed (arrow #3). If we click on the 'Next' button on our example screen we get the following screen. Notice that there is extra room under the last report. This screen can be populated with as many different custom Autosequences that the business requires. A POS professional programmer can add reports to this list or remove ones that the restaurant is no longer using.

POS Lifeline.com

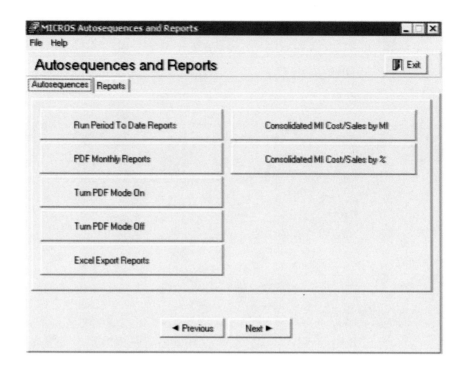

For many restaurants the Autosequence screens are where most of the daily reporting work will be done. If, for example, the restaurant's daily routine is to run the reports the next morning, a manager could access the Autosequences in the morning to run the previous night's sales and labor reports. Likewise if the monthly sales and tax reports have not been set up to run automatically they could easily be run from the Autosequence screen. The power of Autosequences lies in the ability to set the system up to automatically run periodical reports as needed.

## The Reports Tab

The Reports tab is where the manager has access to all of the visible reports that are built into the Micros POS system. These reports do not run automatically. These individual reports must be defined at the time they are run.

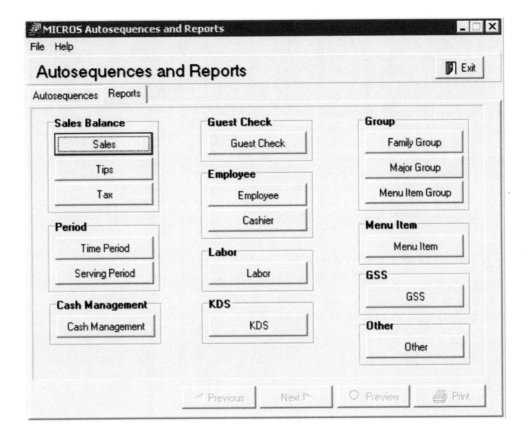

The reports section is divided up into categories. Within the categories are subcategories where appropriate. Micros has hundreds of reports that can be run. By breaking them up into categories it makes it much easier to find the correct report.

In the following example we are looking for the sales information from a specific date for the bar. The example restaurant has two revenue centers – a bar and a café. We want to specify the bar revenue center.

Since we are interested in the Sales of the bar for the given day it makes sense to start in the Sales Balance | Sales categories. (If we had wanted to take a look at how a particular Menu Item sold on that day, however, we would look under Menu Item | Menu Item.)

Click on the Sales Balance | Sales tab. That will bring up a screen that lists the reports that are programmed to appear:

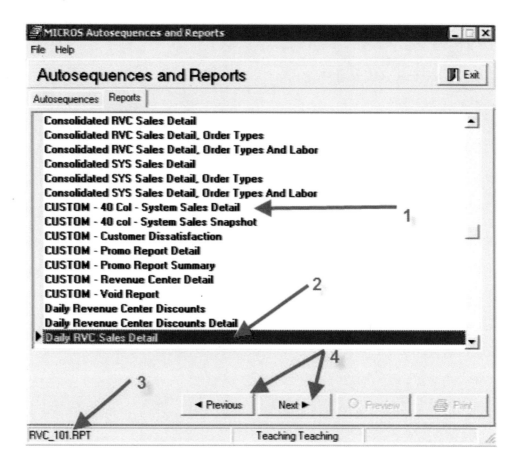

In the example above you can see that there are many reports to choose from in the Sales tab. Each system varies depending on how it was initially set up so if you don't have the same reports listed don't worry.

In the above image notice that some of the reports contain, "40 Col -..." (arrow #1). These reports are specifically programmed for the front of the house or workstations printers.

Notice that the highlighted report shows up inverted in color (arrow #2). The actual name of the report on the system shows up on the lower left of the dialogue box (arrow #3). This can be helpful information when a programmer is trying to set up an Autosequence for the restaurant. Finally, the Previous and Next buttons (arrow #4) allow us to move forward with the selected report or to return to the previous screen where we chose our category.

For our example there is actually more than one report that will give us the information we are looking for. Because we are looking for a specific revenue center's sales on a specific day we could choose either of the two reports below:

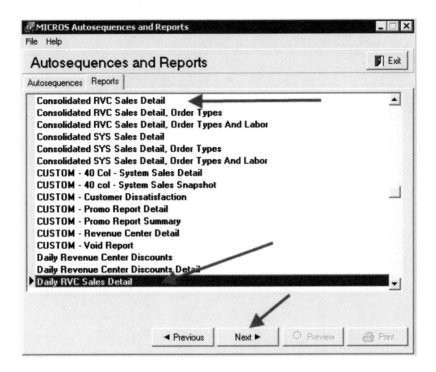

For the sake of our example we will choose the 'Daily RVC Sales Detail' and click on the 'Next' button.

> **TIP**: With so many reports in the Micros POS system, it is often times necessary to explore a few different reports until the correct one is found. Once you've found the appropriate report write down not only the name of the report, but the file name as well. This will make it easier to find at a later date should you need to run it again.

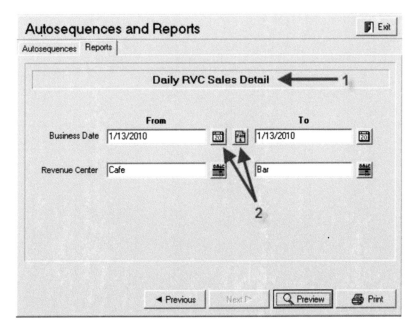

The screen that comes up prompts for certain parameters to be set before the report can be run. These differ depending on the report. At the top of the dialogue box the name of the report is displayed (arrow #1). In the main section of our example the report is prompting for business dates to be set and the revenue center.

There are two ways to set the date. The white button that looks like a calendar will bring up a functioning calendar that lets you select the date.

By selecting the correct month and year from the drop down box you can navigate to the date that you want to look at. In our example we're going to navigate to November 23, 2009. Then click the OK button.

After we set the 'TO' date by using the other white calendar box we will need to select the 'Café' revenue center using the green boxes that look like a bar.

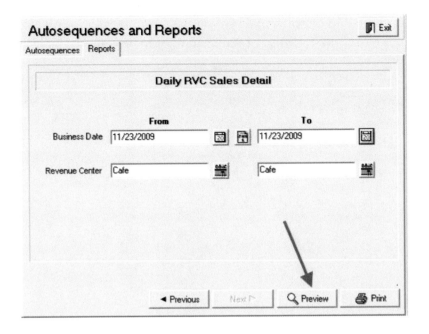

Now that the parameters are set we're ready to click on 'Preview.' This will bring up the Report Viewer with the information that we've requested.

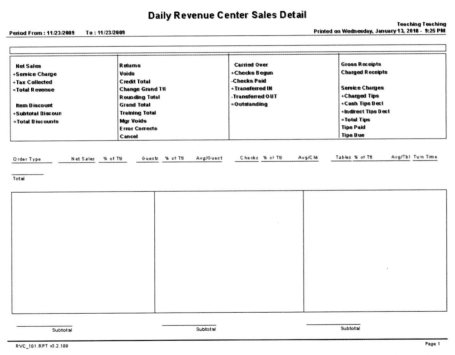

Our report appears empty because the Café in our example was closed on that particular day. Had it been open and busy, the POS System would have populated it with the relevant sales information.

If the report has pulled up the information you were looking for, you can now go to the top and 'Print' it. Once you're finished with the report, click on the 'Close' button. This will take you back to the parameters screen.

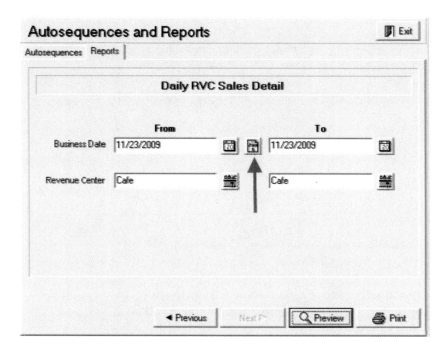

This time let's take a look at that yellow button. The yellow button brings up a list of pre-set date ranges.

If the date range you're looking for meets one of these criteria, choosing this box rather than setting each beginning and end date can significantly speed you up when running multiple reports.

Once you're finished with the report close out of the Report Viewer.

If this was the last report that we needed to run we would simply click on the 'Exit' button.

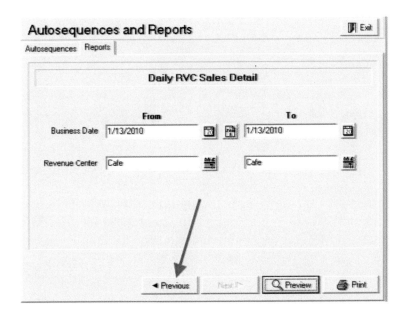

If we needed to run more reports we could click on the 'Previous' button to take us back step by step to the Category list:

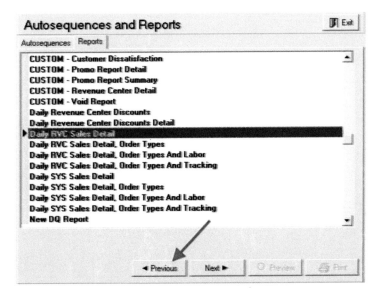

Click the 'Previous' button again and we'll be back at the Category list:

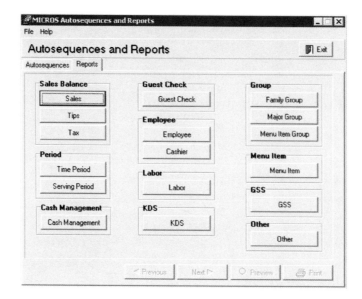

Those are the basics for running reports through the Autosequences and Reports. If you find yourself running the same reports on a consistent basis let your Micros programmer know. Chances are they can program an Autosequence to remove one more step from an already busy day!

# Credit Cards

## Checking the Batch, Manually Creating & Running the Batch

Micros relies on an outside software application to batch the credit card transactions from the night before. This program is called "CreditCards.exe," but should show up on your desktop as a shortcut called, "Credit Card Batch."

It is important that the Office Manager make checking this program once a week part of their routine because there are times when there will be a communication error or duplicate record and a batch will slip through the cracks. It is very rare but does happen.

In this section we will first check to make sure that the batch from the night before has gone through then we will run through how to manually create the batch if it hasn't automatically run. Finally we will look at other applications of the Credit Card Batch program.

## Checking the Credit Card Batch

This is a very quick exercise that should be carried out daily to avoid additional charges from the processor. We begin by locating the program named, "Credit Card Batch." When you double click on it you will be prompted for a password. Enter the same password that you use for POS Configurator. The following screen will come up:

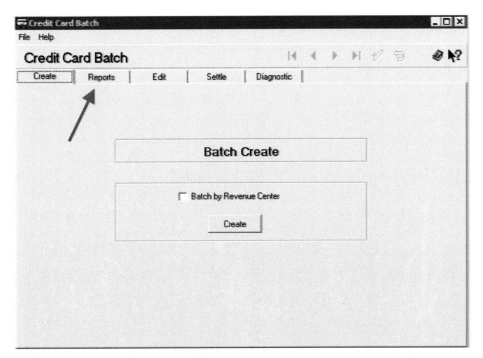

Click on the "Reports" tab. Here you have a list of the batches that stretch back about 6 months (depending on how your system is set up).

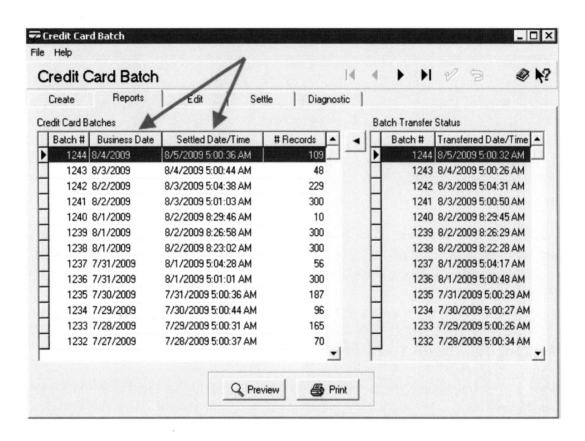

When we are checking to see if the batch went through for a particular day simply check the "Business Date" column and look to the right of the date you're checking to see if it settled. For most restaurant and bar applications the "Settled Date" should be the following day.

That's it! That's all we have to do to verify that a batch was created and settled for any given day.

## Manually Creating and Transferring a Batch

The only time you might need to manually create and transfer a batch is if the system had a power failure the night before or was otherwise unable to communicate with the credit card processor. Upon checking the "Reports" tab you will see that the batch had <u>not</u> been settled. The "Settled Date/Time" field would be blank.

Click on the "Create" tab.

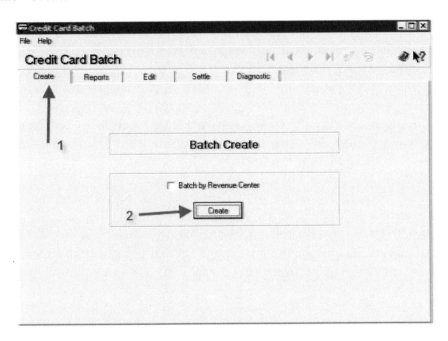

Click the "Create" button. If any credit card entries are found they will be placed in a batch file. This file will be given a name ending with the date.

If there are no entries to add to the batch, it is possible that it has already been created and just needs to be settled. Either way, the next step is the same. Click on the "Settle" tab.

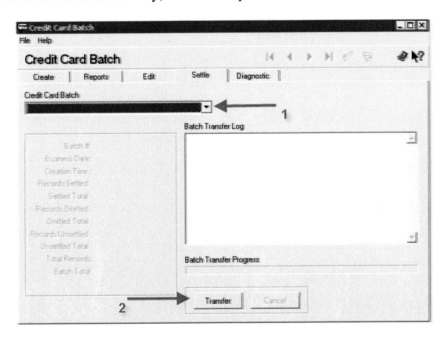

Click on the little drop down arrow next to the field, "Credit Card Batch" (arrow #1). Select the batch you wish to settle and then click on the "Transfer" button (arrow #2).

That's all there is to it!

## Using the Credit Card Batch to Respond to Charge Back Requests

One of the advantages of having the credit card information accessible through the Credit Card Batch program is that it allows you to research what a specific credit card was settled for on any particular night. This is particularly helpful when responding to a charge back request. In addition to displaying totals, it's provides a whole bunch of information to the Office Manager.

Simply go to the "Report" tab within the Credit Card Batch program and double click on the batch that settled the night after the request. This will open up a "Credit Card Batch Detail" that will show you all of the credit cards, the check numbers associated with them, who the server was, base amount, charge tip and time of transaction. This can be very useful information when looking into a problem. It will also allow you to print the batch if necessary.

> ***TIP***: An easier way to respond to charge back requests is to utilize the EJ Organizer. Please see the section titled, "EJ Organizer".

# Manager Procedures – Adjusting Time Cards

## Adjusting Time Cards on the Back Office PC

There are two ways to adjust employee time cards. The first way, and the way this section will cover, is from the back office computer. No matter how the restaurant was set up, you will always be able to access the Manager Procedures from the back office PC. The second way is from any terminal in the restaurant through the manager procedures button. Whether or not you are able to access Manager Procedures from the POS terminals will depend on how the restaurant was initially set up.

The benefit of working with Manager Procedures from the back office PC is that it is much easier to make multiple adjustments to one or many different employees.

For this exercise we will be using a program called, "Manager Procedures." There should be an icon on the desktop for this.

Once opened you will be prompted to enter a password. Swipe in or enter your password manually to get to the home screen:

Once there press the "Employees" button. A list similar to this will appear:

This lists the employees in alphabetical order by last name. Often times the business will have hundreds of employees over time. It is therefore easiest to locate the particular employee we are looking for by using the search box on the bottom of the window.

For this example we're going to search for Training then select JohnDoe from the available employees. We do this by entering the last name in the search box and clicking on the "Go" button next to it (the red arrow above).

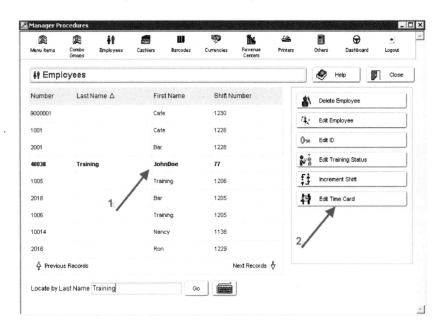

Once you've located the employee click on the employee record to choose it. In the screen shot above you can tell that we've selected JohnDoe Training (arrow #1) because the record is bold compared to the others.

Next click on the "Edit Time Card" button (arrow#2 above). This will take you to a list of the employee's different records. They are listed from most recent on top.

> **NOTE**: Each time an employee clocks in a record is started. Each record has a beginning and an end. If the employee forgets to clock out the system will automatically clock them out and then back in when it runs its end of day procedures. Thereby creating two records that will need to be adjusted.

Click on the record you want to edit and then press the edit button on the bottom left of the screen. Note that when you click on the record it becomes bold.

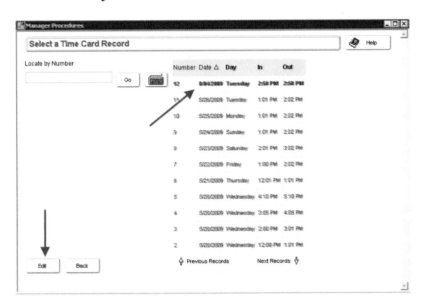

Once the Edit button has been pressed it brings up the particular information for that record. For our example JohnDoe Training forgot to clock in and out for his shift. So we'll need to adjust both his Clock In time and his Clock Out time. We make the changes to each field by clicking on the button to the right of the field.

> **NOTE**: When an employee forgets to clock in there is no record to adjust. Therefore it is necessary to create a record and then adjust it. The easiest way to do this is to look the employee up in POS Configurator. Go to the Security Tab and write down their security number. Clock them in and out manually to create a record.

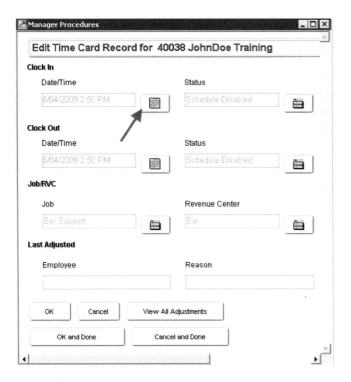

This brings up a screen that allows us to make the necessary changes. Select the correct date and time for the Clock In and then press the "OK" button. For our example JohnDoe should have clocked in at 8pm on the 3$^{rd}$ of August.

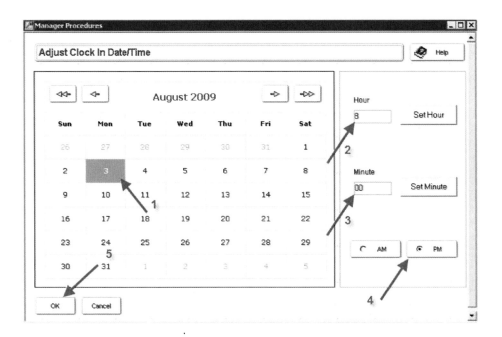

Do the same for the Clock Out time and then press the "OK" button on the bottom of the dialogue box.

> *TIP*: Be careful when adjusting time cards. Always be sure to select the correct AM or PM choice. Failing to do so may give an employee an extra 24 hours of pay. If the system will not move on to the "reason" screen it's probably because the "Time In" and "Time Out" overlap each other. The system will not allow you to move forward if any of the time records overlap.

The POS system will now prompt you for a reason why you are making this change. Select the appropriate reason and press the "OK" button to complete the change.

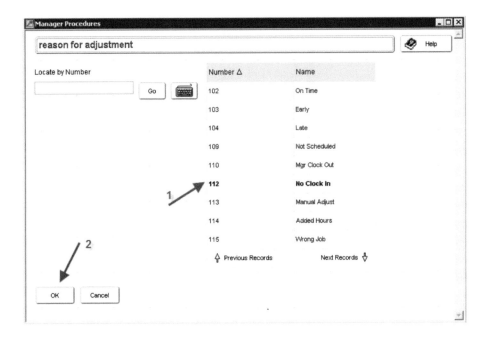

Once you select "OK" it takes you back to list of time card records for this employee. If there are other changes to be made you can simply select the next record to change and go through the process again.

Once you're finished with all the changes to this employee, press the "Cancel" button on the lower left of the dialogue box. Don't worry – you're just going back to the previous screen; the POS has already saved the time card adjustments you've made.

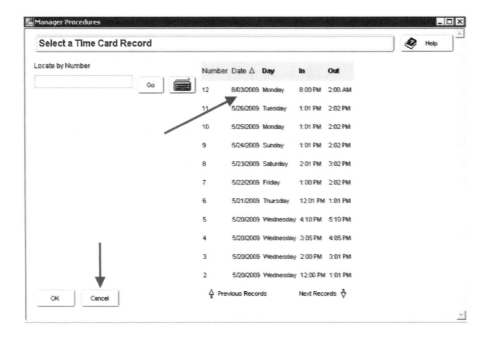

You can see in our example above that the system has made the changes to our Clock In and Clock Out record and now we're ready to go back to the previous screen. Press Cancel. Now press the "Back" button to take you to the list of employees.

Continue editing other employees as needed by following the procedures above for each one.

When you are finished editing time cards you can now exit the program by pressing the "Close" button.

# Transaction Analyzer

Transaction Analyzer is a program that creates reports by polling the transaction detail from the database. It allows you to sort through the data stored in the system based on operator defined fields. It allows the user to set conditions on a search and pulls out the required information. This is useful for tracking contests among the staff or looking for something particular. Please note: Transaction Analyzer only accesses data for the previous 14 days. So if you're running a month long sales contest with the staff it is necessary to run it two or more times throughout the month to track the correct sales data.

## Introduction to Transaction Analyzer

Open up Transaction Analyzer. The Home screen looks like this:

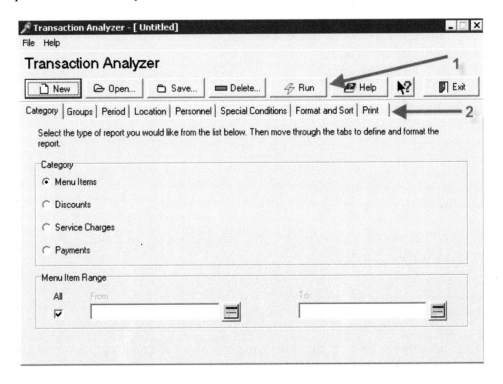

Across the top are 8 buttons (arrow #1). Starting with New and ending in Exit. These buttons allow you to create, save and recall past reports. When you first open Transaction Analyzer it is ready to create a new report from scratch. The group of tabs below (arrow #2) is where we define the parameters of a new report. Working from left to right they are:

## Category

This tab allows us to define the type of sales data we want to search.

## Groups

When creating a report for Menu Items, this tab appears allowing the user to define a Menu Item group, a Family group or a Major group in order to look more closely at a particular item.

## Period

This tab defines a time range. This range can be a date range or a time range.

## Location

This tab allows us to define the revenue center and a group of workstations or one workstation in particular.

## Personnel

Use this tab to define an individual employee or a range of employees.

## Special Conditions

This tab allows the user to enter more specific search criteria utilizing the Wizard or the advanced function.

## Format and Sort

This tab allows the user to select the reporting columns for the report. With this tab you can also define the order in which the information is displayed.

## Print

This tab allows you to set up the way the printer prints the information in the report. Here you can select Portrait or Landscape or to send the report to a file.

# Creating a Report

### Step 1: Category

Working from left to right across the tabs, the first step is to choose the category of the report that is needed.

| | |
|---|---|
| Menu Items | Shows detail by menu items ordered |
| Discounts | Shows detail by discounts applied |
| Service Charges | Shows transaction detail by service charges applied |
| Payments | Shows transaction detail by payments applied |

*Example:* The business has been running a competition among the bartenders to see who could sell the most Blue Moon draft beer for the past week. Therefore the General Manager has asked for a detailed report of how many Blue Moon drafts were sold over the past week by each employee.

Therefore choose 'Menu Items' then in the 'Menu Item Range' in the bottom of the dialogue box click to define the 'From' and 'To' fields for the menu item range.

> *NOTE:* When you choose a category the bottom of the window will change to a range box associated with the category. If 'All' is selected the program will select all of the records for that category and the 'From' and 'To' fields will be disabled. If 'All' is not selected and no records are defined a blank table will be displayed.

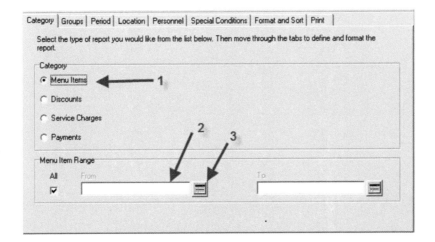

When you click the Data Record button to the right of the field (arrow #3) a list of the database comes up:

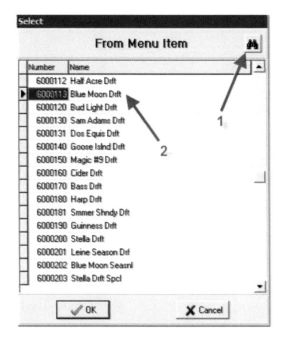

Notice that you can use the find function (the binoculars – arrow #1) to find a particular item in the database rather than having to scroll through the entire database. Once found, highlight it (arrow #2) and click 'OK'.

Do the same for the 'To' field and then click on the second tab, "Groups."

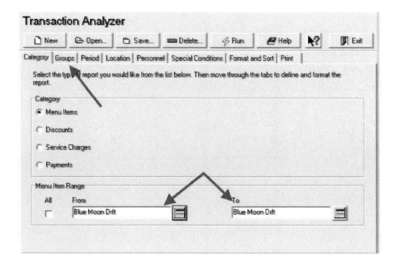

**Step 2: Groups Tab**

The Groups tab is only available when working with Menu Items. This tab is used to specify the particular major, family or menu item group. This allows the report to be as specific or general as required.

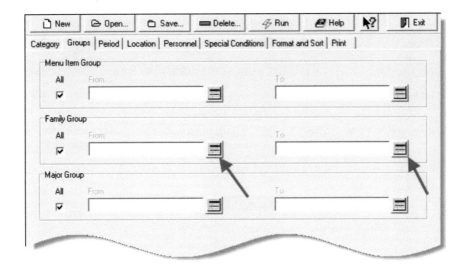

In order to keep the example report concise we would choose the 'Beer Taps' family group because 'Blue Moon' belongs to the "Beer Taps' family group.

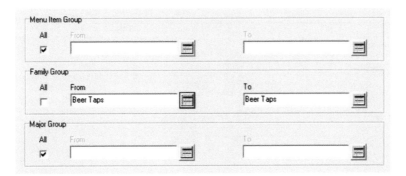

**Step 3: Set the Period**

The 'Period' tab allows the user to look at a broad picture of dates or a specific time period.

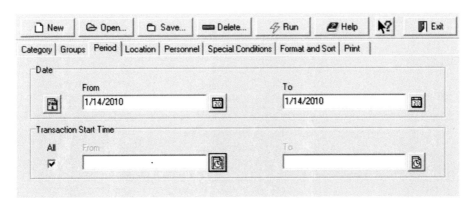

The buttons available are the same as from the POS Configurator and the Autosequences and Reports. You can choose a date by looking it up with the Calendar button ⊞ or choose from pre-set dates with the ▦ button. In addition the ▣ button allows you to set an exact start and end time.

For the example we will use the Preset Date Ranges button to choose the 'Last Week' option.

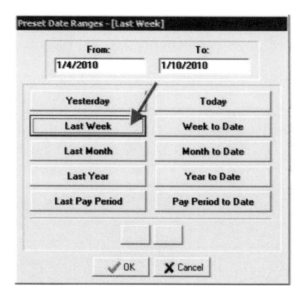

We want the entire day to be selected so we will set the Transaction Start Time on the bottom of the window to 'All.'

> *TIP*: When using the pre-defined date range button the date range will be that specification if the report is saved and used again later.

**Step 4: Location**

Location allows us to look at a particular revenue center or a particular work station within a revenue center. For our example we will set it to look only at the bar revenue center because this contest was only for the bartenders.

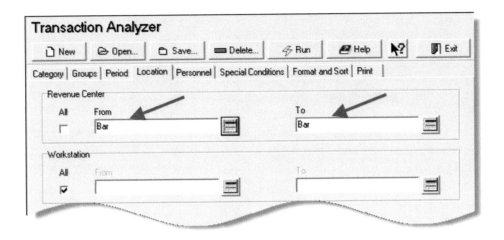

Additionally, we are interested in all the workstations and therefore will leave that set for 'All.'

**Step 5: Personnel**

This tab is used to specify a range of employees or individual employees that meet the search criteria.

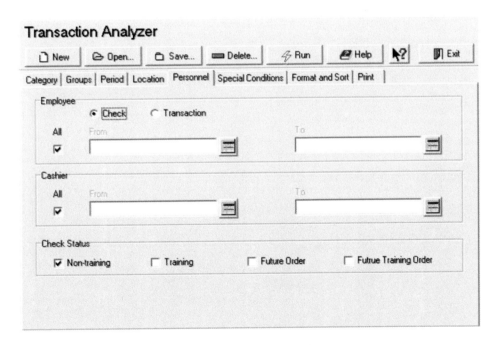

Transaction Analyzer gives you the option of looking at checks or transactions, specific employees or cashiers, and a particular check type.

For our example we're going to specify all employees (cashiers are irrelevant for our application because we don't have any) and Non-training checks.

**Step 6: Special Conditions**

The Special Conditions tab is used to more precisely filter the data that the program will pull out of the database. It allows you to set precise conditions that have to be met in order to filter out some of the unwanted information.

There are two ways to define special conditions. The first is to use the Wizard. This will walk you through the process with assistance. It will ask you questions in an effort to determine what filter factors you wish to add. The second way is to click on the 'Advanced' button on the bottom of the window.

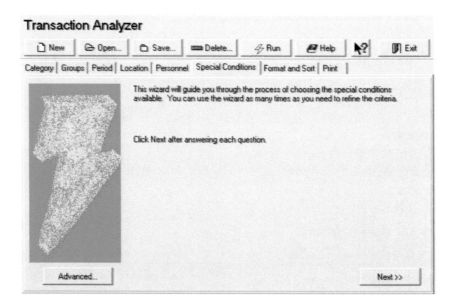

To run the Wizard click on the 'Next>>' button on the lower right.

This will take you trough the Wizard one question at a time.

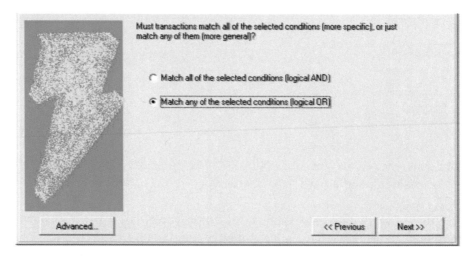

The other way to set special conditions is to click on the 'Advanced' button. This will bring up the following window.

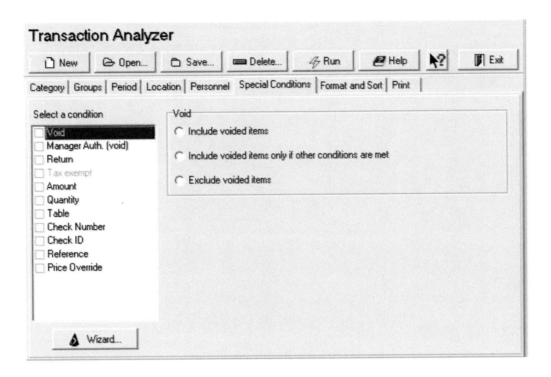

Using the Advanced button allows you to set the same conditions but doesn't walk you through the potential answers. Here you click on a condition on the left and the options for that condition appear in the detail area of the window on the right.

Once the Special Conditions have been set we are ready to move on to the next tab.

> **NOTE**: Special Conditions do not have to be set in order to run the report. They are very useful when looking for very specific data but don't let the process of setting them overwhelm you. When in doubt, skip the special conditions. You can always come back and set them later in order to refine the report.

For our example we will not set any special conditions.

## Step 7: Format and Sort

This step defines what information shows up on the report.

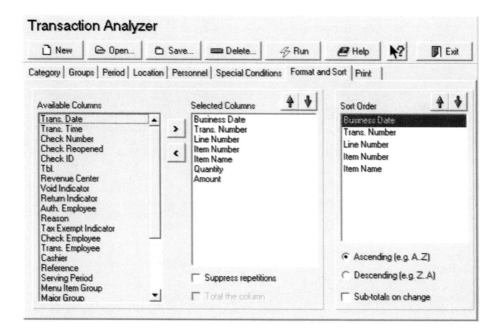

Available Columns – This list shows all of the available columns that can appear on a report.

Selected Columns – This list shows all of columns that have already been selected to show up on the report.

Sort Order – By changing the sort order the order of the columns changes.

By using the right and left arrow keys we can add and remove columns from the report:

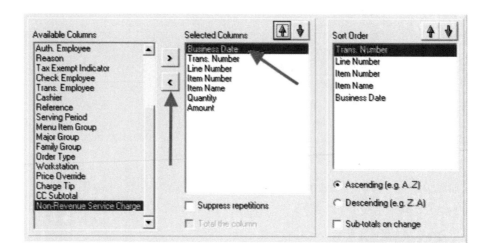

For or example, for instance, we do not need the business date to show up. By highlighting it in the 'Selected Columns' area and clicking on the ◄ arrow button we send it back to the 'Available Columns' and it will no longer be on our report.

For something as simple as our example we only need to know who the 'Check Employee' was, the 'Item Name,' 'Quantity' and 'Amount.'

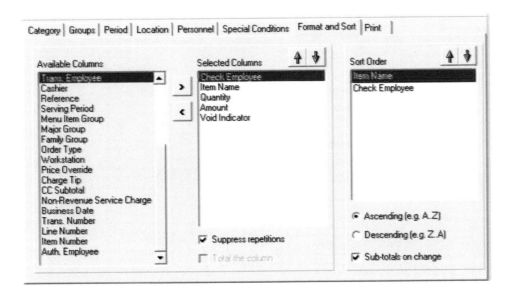

By choosing the 'Suppress Repetitions' under the 'Selected Columns' when we have the 'Check Employee' highlighted we get a cleaner looking report. When all of the criteria have been set, click the Run button at the top of the window:

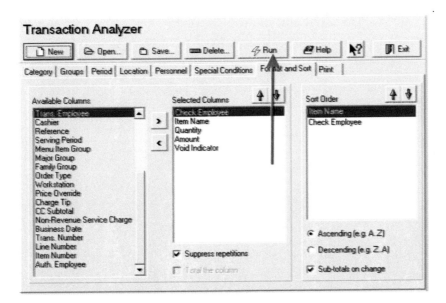

Our example yields the following report:

| Employee | Check<br>Item Name | Quantity | Amount | V<br>I |
|---|---|---|---|---|
| Jason R | Blue Moon Drft | 1 | 4.52 | F |
| | Blue Moon Drft | 1 | 4.52 | F |
| | Blue Moon Drft | 1 | 4.52 | F |
| | Blue Moon Drft | 1 | 4.52 | F |
| Jason T | Blue Moon Drft | 1 | 4.52 | F |
| | Blue Moon Drft | 1 | 4.52 | F |
| | Blue Moon Drft | 1 | 4.52 | F |
| Johnatho | Blue Moon Drft | 1 | 4.52 | F |
| Jon S. | Blue Moon Drft | 1 | 4.52 | F |
| | Blue Moon Drft | 1 | 4.52 | F |
| | Blue Moon Drft | 1 | 4.52 | F |
| Philip R | Blue Moon Drft | 1 | 4.52 | F |
| Ray R | Blue Moon Drft | 1 | 4.52 | F |
| | Blue Moon Drft | 1 | 4.52 | F |
| | Blue Moon Drft | | 4.52 | F |

On the left it lists the Check Employee, then the Item Name, then the Quantity and finally the amount. Notice that the name of the bartender is not repeated for each entry. That's because we set it to 'Suppress Repetitions.'

If you think that the report you have just created will be used in the future be sure to save it using the save button at the top of the window.

This has been a general introduction to Transaction Analyzer. If you find yourself or your management team using the same reports from Transaction Analyzer on a steady basis, contact your Micros POS programming professional. They can set up an Autosequence to run these reports in the background thereby freeing up more time for other tasks.

# EJ Organizer

Every night, as part of the system's auto run utilities, Micros creates a backup ZIP file of the "register tape" for the previous day. This tape includes every check and transaction from the night before. EJ Organizer is designed to be able to look at this register tape and quickly find relevant information.

It can be used numerous ways. Below we will look at how to do the following:

1.   Look up all servers who rang on the register system on a given day
2.   Locate the relevant check for a charge-back rebuttal

## EJ Overview

Open EJ Organizer. The following screen will appear.

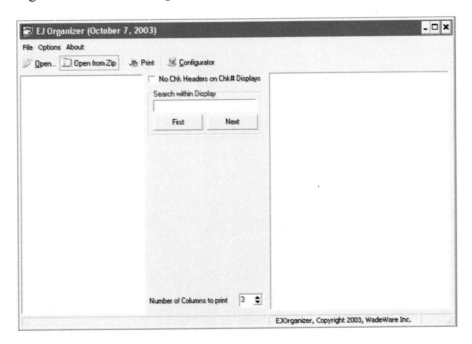

Click on "Open from Zip" The following dialogue box should come up:

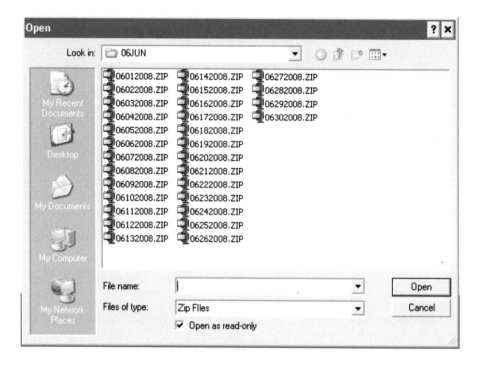

This will usually show the current month's files. By looking in the folder hierarchy you can access previous months and years if necessary. Note that the date of the Zip file is the date of service. If you are "rolling the business day" after midnight, and consequently processing credit cards at the same time, there will be a lag of 1 day between the day of the charge settlement and the day of service. Highlight the relevant day and press the "Open" key.

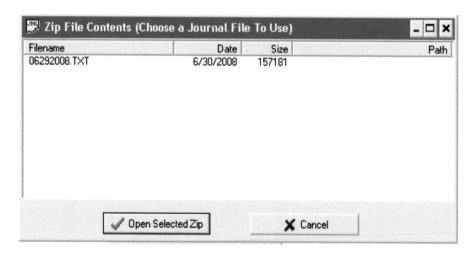

Highlight the file and press the "Open Selected Zip"

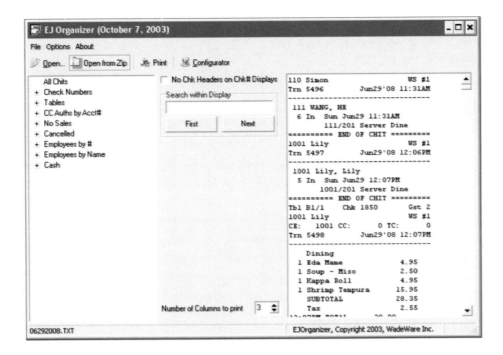

This is the primary screen for the EJ Organizer. On the left are the headers. These allow the user to quickly navigate to the information they are searching for. On the right is the detail box. This will always list the information, in exacting detail, of whichever header is selected.

## Example 1: Who rang on the register?

In order to see who rang on the registers for the day in question, the user would go to the left side of the screen, where it says, "Employees by Name" and click on the plus sign. This will bring up a list of all employees that started a check on the system on that given day.

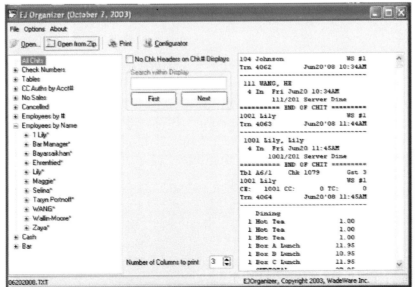

Let's say that upon review, the employee "Maggie" wasn't scheduled and should not have been ringing. By clicking on the plus sign next to her name we're able to bring up all the checks that were run under Maggie's identity.

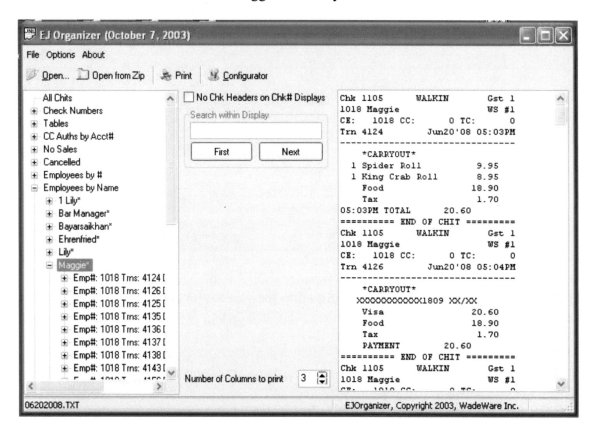

Looking in the right window, we're able to see when the checks were rung, what tables they were for, etc. Utilizing this information it becomes easier to identify problems and potential abuse of the system by an employee.

## Example 2: Responding to a charge-back request

You have received a chargeback request for a credit card that processed on June 21$^{st}$, 2008. The last four digits of the credit card are 0973. Opening the June 20th Zip file, we go to the "CCAuths by Account #" on the left side. Click on the plus sign and look for the last four digits of 0973. Double click on that line.

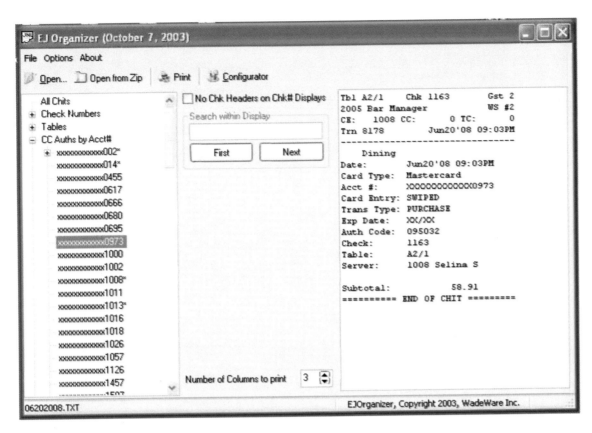

Looking at the check on the right, we can see that it's check number 1163. The next step is to click on the plus sign next to the "CC Auths by Acct#" in order to close it. Then click on the plus sign next to "Check Numbers."

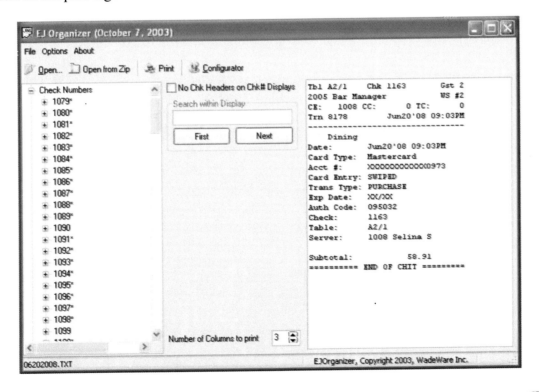

Find check # 1163 and double click on it.

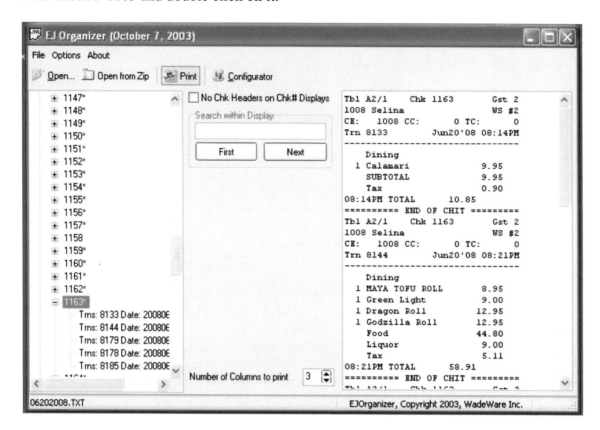

Notice on the right side, in the detailed information box, that the scroll arrow indicates that there is more information for this check then can be seen at any given time. This information box has everything that was rung on the check.

Having this information for the CC processing company will almost always guarantee success for a chargeback rebuttal.

Open the Microsoft "Notepad" program. There should be a shortcut for it on the desktop.

Placing the mouse in the upper left corner of the information box of the EJ Organizer, highlight all the information by dragging the mouse down. With the information highlighted, press CTRL-C (for copy). Now click in the open window of the Notepad and press CTRL-V (for paste). All of the information from the detail box should now look like this in the Notepad program.

Go to the File Menu and click on "Save As"

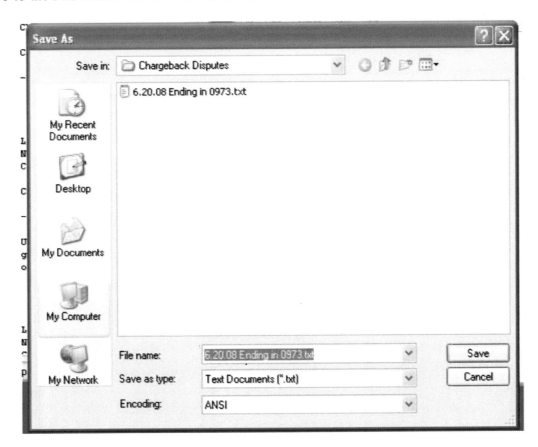

Here you'll notice that I've saved it by naming it the date of the transaction followed by the last four digits of the credit card number. This will help you locate it in the future. We've also saved it in a folder on the desktop named, "Chargeback Disputes."

The final steps to take are to print out a copy, find the credit card slip and fax that information to the credit card processor.

Be sure to save your Notepad file and close both the Notepad and the EJ Organizer programs.

# Manager Front of House Procedures

## Using the Work Station

86-ing an item
Adjusting timecards
Assigning a swipe card
Running server and bartender reports
Running an open check report
Changing the kitchen theme
Editing closed checks
Adjusting payment type on a transaction
Transferring Checks
Splitting Checks
Multiple payments on a single check

# Manager Front of House Training

## How to Change a Menu Item & Pricing Using Manager Procedures

In the following exercise we will explore how to make simple adjustments to a dedicated "Specials" menu item button. These adjustments will allow the system to prompt for the correct information for any given menu item. In particular we will look at how to change price as well as how to define which "Required Condiments" the system asks for from the servers.

To begin, swipe in with the Manager Card. The screen will look like this:

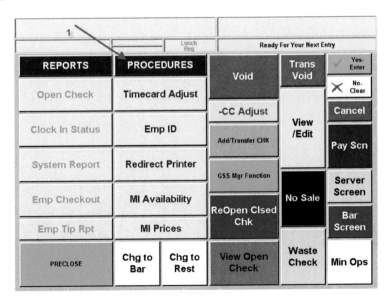

Press the brown "Procedures" button at the top. On the next screen press the "Menu Items" button. (Shown below with the red arrow #1 pointing to it).

This will bring up the following menu items screen:

Now we must locate the item we are going to change. Press the keyboard button.

POS Lifeline.com

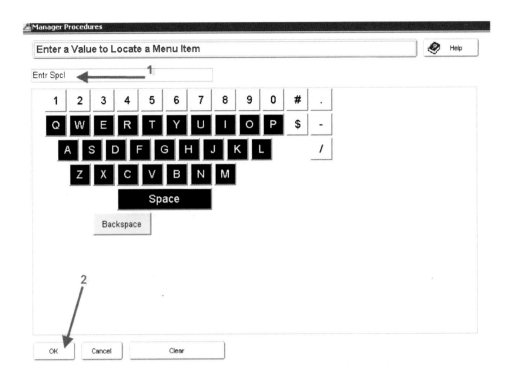

Type the name of the menu item in and press the "OK" button. For this example we're going to be searching for, "Entr Spcl."

Once it locates items with similar names, select the item you want and then press the "Edit Menu Item" button.

Select the "Condiments" tab. Shown above with the arrow.

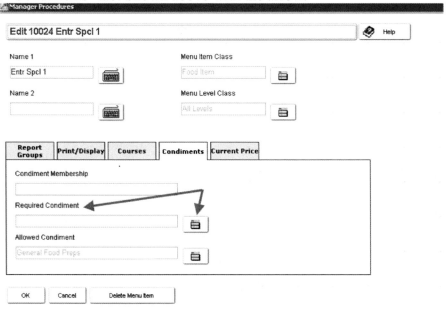

The first thing we want to edit is the "Required Condiment." This is where we tell the computer what information to ask the servers for. If this were a meat dish.we might want the computer to ask us for a temperature to cook the meat to. If it were a fish dish we might want the computer to ask us for a preparation style (blackened, grilled, etc.). For the sake of this example, let's assume it's a fish dish that will require the server to enter a

preparation and one side dish. Press the button to the right of the "Required Condiment" field. See above with the red arrow to the right.

Micros will now prompt you for the correct required condiment:

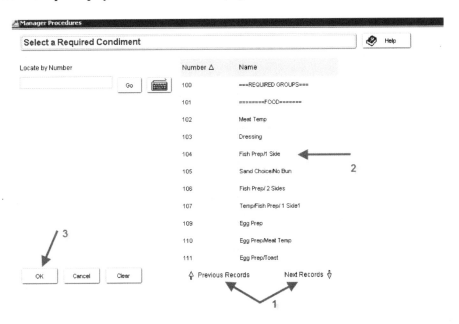

Search through the list (using the buttons that the red arrows (#1) are pointing to above). Once you find the correct one, highlight it (arrow #2) and then press the "OK" button. Micros takes you back to the previous screen and now you can see that the computer will now prompt for a "Fish Prep / 1 Side."

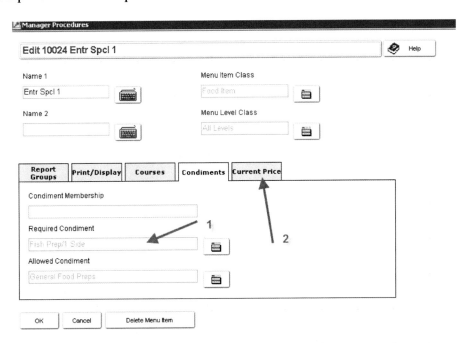

Now we need to change the price. Click on the "Current Price" tab. Shown above with arrow #2.

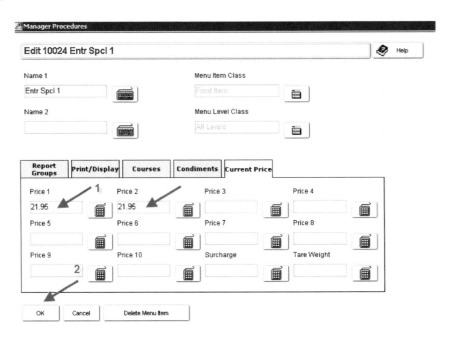

It will be necessary to change both the "Price 1" and "Price 2" fields. We do this by

pressing the ![button] button and entering the new price. Once we are done entering the new prices, press the "OK" button.

This will take you back out to the Menu Items list. From here you can change more items or simply press the "Close" button.

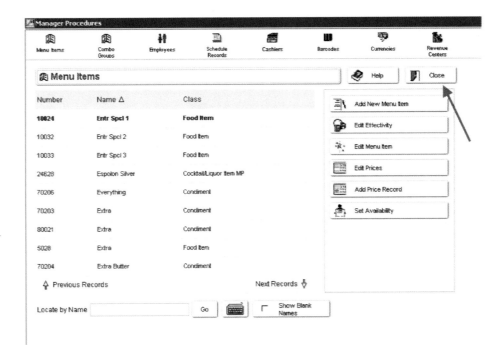

Congratulations! You've just modified the two most important aspects of the menu item: the price and the required condiments.

# Section 3: General Information

# Setting the Default Printer (Windows XP)

Put the mouse over the lower left corner where the "Start" button is:

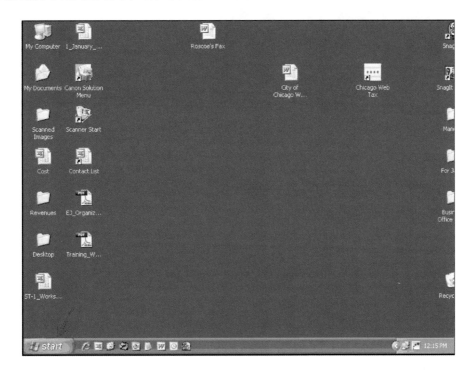

Click on the left mouse button. It should look like this:

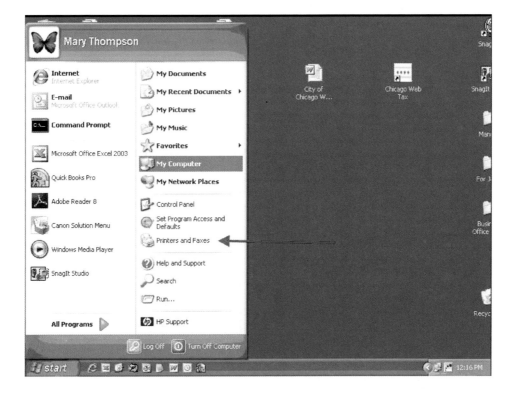

Now highlight the "Printers and Faxes" button and click the left mouse button.

A screen similar to this will appear listing the printers on your system.

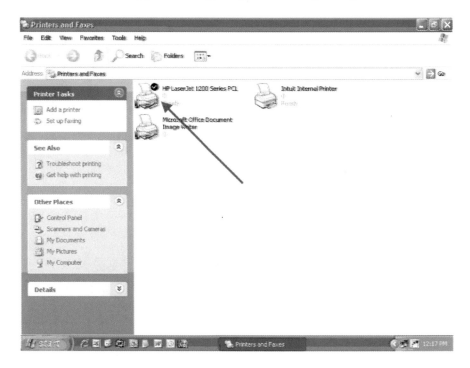

Notice in the image above the printer the red arrow is pointing at. This printer has a little check mark before its name. This means it is set as the Default Printer. If the printer you are using or want to use doesn't have this little check mark next to it do the following. Right click on the printer you want to set as the default printer.

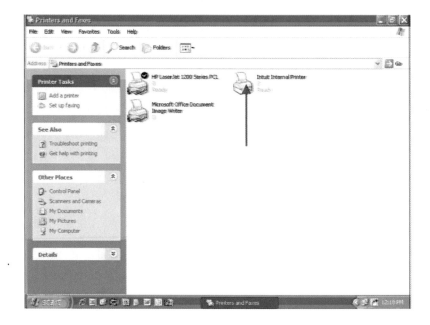

When you right click on it, it should look like this:

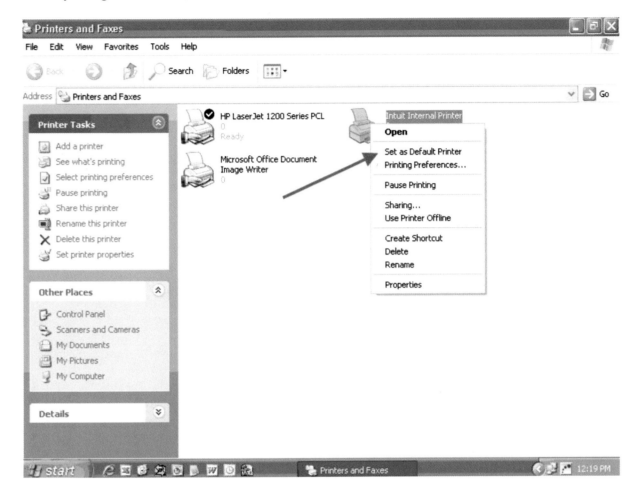

Move your cursor over the line that says, "Set as Default Printer" and click the left mouse button.

You have now just set your printer to be the default printer on the system.

Made in the USA
Las Vegas, NV
05 January 2023

65057069R00107